BOUNDARIES
& BREAKING CYCLES OF PAIN

HEALING THE ROOTED PAIN OF VICTIM, PERPETRATOR, AND RESCUER ROLES

STEPHANIE TUCKER

Boundaries and Breaking Cycles of Pain
By Stephanie Tucker
ISBN: 978-1-936451-10-4

© 2025 Spirit of Life Recovery, Inc. All Rights Reserved.

Permissions and Copyright Notice

Please do not distribute this material without written consent. All proceeds from this course directly support our nonprofit mission. We kindly ask you to support this ministry by encouraging others to purchase their own copy of this resource.

This publication is protected under U.S. copyright laws. Except as permitted under the Copyright Act of 1976, no part of this book may be reproduced, distributed, or transmitted in any form or by any means, including electronic or mechanical methods, or stored in a retrieval system, without prior written permission from the publisher, Spirit of Life Recovery.

An exception is granted to the sole purchaser of this book: you may photocopy worksheets or pages for *personal use only*. These materials may not be shared, reproduced, or distributed to others in any form.

Bible Translation Credits

All Scripture quotations are taken from the New Living Translation (NLT*, ©1996, 2004, 2015 by Tyndale House Foundation. Used by permission of Tyndale House Publishers, Inc., Carol Stream, Illinois 60188. All rights reserved.

Additional translations used include:
New International Version (NIV), Holy Bible, New International Version®, NIV® Copyright ©1973, 1978, 1984, 2011 by Biblica, Inc.® Used by permission. All rights reserved worldwide.
The Passion Translation (TPT), © 2017, 2018, 2020 by Passion & Fire Ministries, Inc. Used by permission. All rights reserved.
The Message (MSG), © 1993, 2002, 2018 by Eugene H. Peterson. Used by permission of NavPress. All rights reserved.

Where multiple versions are used for clarity, the translation will be noted following the Scripture reference.

This material is not intended to diagnose, treat, or cure medical, psychological, or psychiatric conditions. If you are in a crisis or facing a life-threatening situation, please seek professional help immediately.

This book is not a substitute for licensed counseling or medical care. Rather, it is offered as a faith-based resource combining biblical principles, personal reflection, and practical tools to support your healing journey. The content shared here is the result of personal experience, biblical study, prayer, professional learning, and various teachings and resources gathered over the years. Every effort has been made to ensure originality and honor the work of others. If you notice any editorial errors or have concerns about the material, please contact the publisher directly.

Printed in the United States of America

Copyright Spirit of Life Recovery. All Rights Reserved.

TABLE OF CONTENTS
Boundaries & Breaking Cycles of Pain

PART ONE: CYCLES OF PAIN .... PAGE 5

PART TWO: GRACE AND SHAME .... PAGE 21

PART THREE: HEALING CYCLES OF PAIN .... PAGE 33

PART FOUR: POWER BOUNDARIES .... PAGE 49

PART FIVE: RESOLUTIONS .... PAGE 67

PART SIX: MADE FOR MORE .... PAGE 81

PART 1
Defining Cycles of Pain

Each of us operates through an internal relationship system that shapes how we interact with ourselves, others, and God. This system includes internal pathways formed by our needs, beliefs, ideals, expectations, and the patterns we've learned over time—patterns of thoughts, feelings, and behaviors. When something in life happens, we respond instinctively. This means we already have a built-in boundary system in place, whether we realize it or not.

These pathways and boundaries are formed in our hearts much like a factory runs a production line. Specific ingredients go in—such as past experiences, emotional needs, and learned responses—and a certain outcome is produced. This process becomes so repetitive that we often respond without even thinking. When the system is healthy, this automatic flow works in our favor, helping us navigate life with strength and confidence. But when negative ingredients—like unresolved pain, unmet needs, or fear—are part of the process, the result can be lifelong cycles of dysfunction, trapping us in familiar but harmful patterns.

Assessing our relationship system helps us understand these automatic responses we've picked up along the way. Think of them as different "modes" we shift into when certain emotional "buttons" get pressed. These modes are not random—they tell a story. When we feel powerless or triggered by past pain, we tend to react by fixing, hiding, fighting, or running. These are survival responses we've used to feel safe, in control, or protected. But over time, they can become limiting and even harmful.

The game changer comes when we allow God to intercept these patterns. Instead of falling back into the same mindsets, He brings something entirely new—His power to restore, transform, and make us whole. Psychology can help us understand our brokenness, but it is the grace and redemption of God that actually sets us free. Through His intervention, our internal systems are re-calibrated, and we are invited into a new way of being—one that breaks the cycles of the past and opens us up to a future full of hope and healing.

This material is meant to help identify the faulty relational cycles we carry that cause us to repeat the same patterns over and over again. As we uncover these cycles, we begin to move toward solutions. Although we will eventually focus on developing healthy boundaries, we'll make other important stops along the way. We'll explore the adaptive roles we've taken on, identify the roots of relational pain, encounter the redemptive power of grace, and allow God to heal our hearts. From there, boundaries are no longer a reaction—they are the natural outcome of real, internal transformation.

While you are free to read this at one time, it is something that you will learn as much throughout your day as you do learning it in your head. Relearning requires that we unlearn, and that takes

Copyright Spirit of Life Recovery. All Rights Reserved.

a level of intentionality. But above all else, our greatest need is to acquire grace. In this workshop you will:

- Define the adaptive roles of victim, perpetrator and rescuer
- Understand the power of shame and how it instigates broken cycles
- Learn about the resource of grace and what it does to birth change and hope
- Explore the pain and the roots of your story, understanding original pain
- Apply grace to relationships with others
- Build power boundaries, bridges and exit strategies
- Understand how to resolve conflict to build healthier relational pathways.

VICTIM, PERPETRATOR AND RESCUER CYCLES

For the purposes of this assessment, we're going to explore three key roles that often show up within painful relational cycles—patterns that many of us have unknowingly participated in but want to break. These roles are commonly referred to as the victim, perpetrator, and rescuer. As you begin to examine them, it's important to resist the urge to judge yourself—or anyone else—for falling into these roles. Instead, try to take on the posture of a gentle observer. These roles are not about identity but about response. They point to the deep pain, fear, and unmet needs we've carried, often since childhood.

In the world of psychology, this dynamic is referred to as the "Drama Triangle," a foundational concept used to identify patterns of dysfunction in relationships. These three roles form an unhealthy loop that feeds on emotional imbalance, shame, and power struggles. It's important to know that these roles are not always dramatic or extreme. They exist on a spectrum. You may notice these patterns in subtle everyday interactions, or in more obvious and painful moments. The examples you'll encounter may feel intense at times, but they are written to help bring clarity and awareness. See these roles not as boxes to fit into, but as broad frameworks that help make sense of internal and relational dynamics.

Remember, these roles do not define you. They are not permanent. They are not your true name. They are coping mechanisms—imperfect and often unhelpful—but rooted in something very human: the need to feel safe, connected, and loved. Psychology gives us helpful tools to understand our behavior, but we're going one step further. We'll also be viewing these roles through a spiritual lens—one that leads us not just to insight, but to transformation through the power of grace.

One of the most difficult realities of these roles is how they tend to sustain each other. They're interdependent. The more we play one role, the more likely others around us will fall into theirs. And what's even more complex is that we rarely stay in just one role. In fact, most of us move through all three depending on the relationship or the situation. In one moment, you may feel like a victim; in another, you may respond by lashing out, taking on the perpetrator role. You might try to rescue someone, only to feel abandoned when they don't do the same for you. This is why these roles are best understood not as judgments we place on others, but as patterns that live within each of us in different ways.

What makes these patterns especially painful is that they are all rooted in shame. Each one reflects a unique strategy for managing pain and powerlessness. These roles are formed in our wounded places—places where we didn't receive what we needed, where our sense of safety or worth was fractured. Many of these patterns are formed early in life, during formative years when we lacked the resources to make sense of what was happening to us. Instead of learning to process pain in healthy ways, we learned to survive. Over time, that survival instinct hardened into relational habits—ways of coping, defending, controlling, or withdrawing that no longer serve us well.

Because these patterns become so familiar, we tend to interpret them through a moral lens—labeling them as "good" or "bad." But that's not how God sees them. These roles are not about morality; they're about pain. While God needs our hearts to receive the grace and forgiveness needed, He does so with a perspective of compassion.

What's most devastating about these roles is that they keep us from the very thing we were made for: deep, secure, loving connection—with God, with others, and even with ourselves. These roles act like impostors. They wear masks of strength, kindness, or control, but underneath they are driven by fear and self-protection. They may imitate care, but often they are rooted in power dynamics or attempts to manage pain rather than truly connect. This doesn't mean we are broken beyond hope. It simply means we are carrying burdens we were never meant to carry alone.

These patterns are not permanent. They are not your final story. When we begin to recognize them, we can begin to interrupt them. When we bring them into the light, they lose their grip. We were never meant to live from shame, fear, or dysfunction. We were created to live from a secure identity as sons and daughters of the living God. In Him, we are not defined by our past or our pain—we are defined by love, purpose, and grace. He doesn't shame us for the roles we've played. He meets us in them. And then, with gentleness, He leads us out.

Healing isn't only possible—it's part of your inheritance. God doesn't waste our pain. He works within it, around it, and even through it, weaving redemption into every chapter of our story. While the process of facing these patterns can feel uncomfortable or even painful at times, it is also sacred. It's how we reclaim our hearts. It's how we return home.

ROLE #1 CYCLE OF PAIN: VICTIM

The first and perhaps most foundational role in the cycle of pain is the victim. This is where most of our personal and relational healing begins because, at some point in life, we have all been a victim. A victim is someone who has been hurt, harmed, or neglected—often by someone else's choices or by a painful circumstance beyond their control. While the degree and exposure of victimization vary greatly, the impact it leaves on the soul is always deeply personal and real.

If we were to rewind the tape of our life, we would see moments—people, words, and experiences—that left lasting imprints of pain. Some of us had help in those moments—someone who saw us, comforted us, or taught us to process grief and move forward. Others were left to carry their pain alone, with no relief, no validation, no one to say, "What happened to you matters."

These original wounds—especially those formed in childhood—often cut the deepest. They shape the way we think, see the world, and view ourselves. Children are inherently vulnerable. When their environments fail to provide love, protection, and value, fear and shame take root. The result is an insecure foundation, often carried into adulthood, marked by the belief that something is inherently wrong with them. Emotional armor becomes necessary. A child learns to protect their heart at all costs.

Living from that kind of foundation is tragic. It can fracture a person's sense of self before they've even had a chance to make empowered choices. That's why the victim role isn't just a behavior pattern—it's a reflection of real wounds. And it's not a mark of weakness. It is evidence of deep hurt that often cannot be explained in words. Yet this space, as painful as it is, holds the door to healing.

VICTIM IN RELATIONSHIPS

The relational strife of a victim is that they often carry a defensive perception in most situations, viewing others through a lens of self-protection. When they sense that someone might be hurtful, they may create distance or make inaccurate assumptions. This defense mechanism can lead to judgment, cynicism, and misinterpretations—all of which complicate relationships.

The victim is also often on the hunt for a hero—someone to be the strength they feel they lack, someone who can right the wrongs and love them in the places where they feel unlovable. When they perceive someone as having the potential to bring healing or support, they may let them in carelessly. Like inviting a thief into their home, this can lead to deeper hurt. Alternatively, they may place such intense emotional need and expectation on a person that the person eventually pulls away. This reactivates the cycle of rejection and reinforces the belief that they are unlovable.

Some victims, too, hold tightly to their identity as a victim in order to maintain a moral stance—as the "good" one amid the chaos of "bad" people and painful circumstances. Being the wounded one gives them a sense of moral clarity in the face of injustice. And while there is often legitimate pain and a valid need for healing, a false sense of morality or superiority can subtly take root. Over time, this dynamic creates more relational fractures, especially when one's sense of "goodness" is positioned against someone else's "badness."

Ultimately, the behaviors of the victim are not about manipulation—they are weapons forged in pain, created to survive. While these responses may not be healthy, they are deeply human. And they make sense in light of the wounds that shaped them.

WHEN YOU'RE IN RELATIONSHIP WITH A VICTIM

Being in a relationship with someone operating from a victim mindset can be incredibly challenging. It can feel like walking on eggshells—constantly defending your intentions or being misunderstood despite your best efforts. Sometimes, you may be cast as the villain simply for offering a different perspective or encouraging accountability.

In those moments, it's tempting to withdraw, retaliate, or overcompensate. But what's needed is clarity—and boundaries on your end, too. We'll explore how to walk this line with compassion and strength later. For now, remember this: the victim's reactions are rarely about you personally. They are responses to unhealed pain that predates your presence.

PATTERNS OF THE VICTIM ROLE

- Powerlessness – Believing life is happening to you and that you have no real choice or agency.
- Blame and resentment – Focusing on what others did wrong rather than your own growth or response.
- Need for rescue – Expecting others to fix, rescue, or emotionally validate you.
- Fear of boundaries – Struggling to say no, express needs, or protect your emotional space.
- Over-identification with pain – Defining yourself by past wounds rather than healing or hope.
- Emotional dependency – Relying on others' approval or presence to feel okay.
- Chronic self-doubt – Feeling stuck, helpless, or unworthy of change.
- Silent suffering – Withholding your true emotions while appearing strong or agreeable.

BOUNDARIES

Victims often struggle deeply with boundaries—both externally and internally. Externally, they may not know how to say no, how to express their needs, or how to define what is and isn't acceptable in relationships. They may allow others to take advantage of them out of fear of being rejected, abandoned, or seen as selfish. Their sense of self-worth is often so fragile that enforcing a boundary feels like risking connection altogether. As a result, they may tolerate mistreatment, overextend themselves, or remain silent in the face of discomfort—believing that their needs are less important than the needs of others.

Internally, the struggle with boundaries is even more subtle and painful. Victims often carry a pervasive sense of invisibility and powerlessness. They don't just feel misunderstood—they feel unseen. There is a quiet belief that their voice doesn't matter, that speaking up will only lead to rejection or conflict, or that no one will truly understand them anyway. This internalized powerlessness causes them to constantly second-guess their feelings, minimize their own pain, and override their intuition in order to keep the peace.

Victims live in a state of emotional bracing, as though always waiting for the next disappointment, betrayal, or outburst. Their nervous system is on high alert, even when nothing is happening on the surface. Trust feels dangerous, and vulnerability feels like exposure. What began as self-protection—necessary in moments of real harm—eventually becomes a prison. The strategies they once used to survive now isolate them from true intimacy.

Over time, the emotional mask becomes harder to take off. They smile while hurting. They show up for others while quietly falling apart inside. They read between the lines of every conversation, searching for hidden messages or threats. Deep down, insecurity rules their internal world. Fear, shame, and a chronic sense of being unloved form their emotional baseline, coloring how they interpret every interaction. Even kind gestures can be met with suspicion, and the absence of reassurance feels like abandonment.

The boundary wounds of the victim go beyond behavior—they are rooted in identity. Without healing, the person begins to believe that they are not worthy of protection, advocacy, or even peace. But healing begins when they realize: they are allowed to take up space. They are allowed to have needs. They are allowed to say no without guilt. And most of all, they are allowed to be seen.

DEEP HEALING

At the heart of every victim's journey is a deep desire not only to be free from pain but to be restored to power, to be seen, and to have unmet needs acknowledged and fulfilled. But before healing can fully unfold in the present, the wounds of the past must be brought into the light—seen, named, and honored for the weight they carry.

A victim doesn't simply need comfort—they need transformation. And that transformation begins with healing the original wounds. These early injuries—often formed when we were most vulnerable—become the lens through which we interpret love, define connection, and assess our own value. If left unhealed, they create internal maps that guide future interactions, often steering us into the same painful patterns again and again.

To heal, there must be a conscious separation between the past and the present. When old wounds are projected onto new situations, we get stuck in cycles of fear, overreaction, and self-sabotage. We may reach for temporary coping mechanisms—approval seeking, performance, emotional suppression—but these are only coverings. They delay healing instead of igniting it. That's why systemic healing—the kind that goes to the root rather than merely treating symptoms—is essential.

TRAUMA IN THE BRAIN AND BODY

Unprocessed pain doesn't just linger in our thoughts—it takes up residence in the body and nervous system. What was once naturally wired for connection and trust begins to function through the lens of fear, anticipation, and protection. Over time, the brain adapts to what it has endured, and the body learns to brace for what it cannot predict. A person may not even realize it, but their system becomes constantly alert, uncertain of what is safe or secure.

In response, the mind may begin to shut down emotions that feel too overwhelming to process. Many learn to overextend care to others while bypassing their own needs, or try to manage the emotions of those around them in hopes of creating a sense of internal calm. In more intense expressions, pain can show up as irritability, emotional withdrawal, controlling behaviors, or even outbursts. These are not signs of weakness or failure—they are deeply patterned strategies the nervous system has learned to survive environments that once felt unsafe.

But safety isn't just something we find outside of us—it's something that must be rebuilt within. Healing begins when the body and soul experience the felt sense that it's okay to rest. This is where grace steps in. In the presence of Jesus, grace is not only a spiritual reality—it becomes a nervous system reality. It slows the inner alarms, quiets the chaos, and gently tells the soul: you are safe now. You don't have to live in defense mode. You can come home to yourself.

WHAT GOD SEES

The most comforting truth in all of this is that God sees the victim fully. He sees the backstory, the hidden pain, the unmet needs, and the silent cries. He sees not only the behavior, but the brokenness beneath it—and He responds with compassion.

Yet God's grace doesn't just offer comfort—it offers power. Power to break cycles. Power to reclaim identity. Power to step out of the shadows and into wholeness.

While we are all accountable for how we respond to life, God's mercy takes into account the whole picture. He knows the influence of trauma, the confusion of early experiences, and the ways we've tried to survive. And He doesn't leave us there.

Through His presence and power, victims are not only comforted—they are rebuilt. God doesn't patch up our pain; He restores us to purpose. His grace offers us a new beginning—one rooted in truth, strength, and love that cannot be shaken.

Awareness brings insight. It reveals where our pain is rooted and how it shapes our relationships, our decisions, and our sense of identity. It opens the door to transformation—the moment we begin to reclaim our voice, recognize our value, and lay down the powerless identity that was never meant to define us.

#2 ROLE CYCLE OF PAIN: THE PERPETRATOR

The perpetrator lies on the other side of the victim's wounds. In many cases, the perpetrator is an external figure—someone who has caused pain, inflicted harm, or violated boundaries. But often, the perpetrator is also internal. It represents the fighter within—a part of us that rises up to protect, to push back, and to prevent further injury. This inner fighter develops in response to past experiences of feeling powerless or unsafe. Its goal is survival through strength.

The fight response isn't inherently wrong. In moments of real threat, the fight mode serves as a God-given response, flooding the body with adrenaline so we can protect ourselves. But this reaction is meant for emergencies, not for daily living. When someone remains in fight mode long after the original danger has passed, it becomes a lifestyle.

Perpetrators live as though every person and every situation is a threat. Strength becomes a shield, and control becomes the method of protection. In this distorted system, power is seen as safety, and weakness is equated with danger. Many who embody this role have experienced intense power struggles in their past and have made an inner vow: never again will I be weak.

Copyright Spirit of Life Recovery. All Rights Reserved.

UNDERSTANDING PERPETRATORS

Perpetrators often emerge in two general expressions: aggressive and passive. While their behaviors may differ on the surface, both operate from underlying pain, insecurity, and a need for control. These patterns are not always rooted in cruelty; they are often the product of unprocessed trauma, distorted beliefs, and learned survival responses.

Aggressive perpetrators are typically loud, dominating, and forceful. They may lash out with anger, blame, or abuse, driven by emotional chaos and under-regulation. Their behavior often reflects a deep internal disconnect—using force, intimidation, or control as protection against perceived vulnerability. Over time, they may grow emotionally numb, their hearts hardened by shame and disconnection.

Though their actions can be deeply damaging, these individuals are often functioning from survival rather than intentional malice. They have been conditioned to equate strength with safety and may see people not as partners, but as threats or tools.

Common behaviors of aggressive perpetrators include:
- Yelling, name-calling, or mocking to dominate
- Using guilt, gas-lighting, or silence to manipulate
- Threatening or intimidating to control
- Physically asserting power or instilling fear
- Twisting Scripture or faith to suppress others
- Controlling decisions and rejecting input
- Isolating loved ones from support
- Punishing through silence, shame, or harsh correction
- Withholding resources to maintain control
- Monitoring, accusing, or restricting out of jealousy or fear

In contrast, passive perpetrators use more covert strategies. Often seen as generous, helpful, or spiritual, they may appear kind on the surface—especially in caregiving roles, churches, or leadership. But beneath the polished exterior lies a quiet need to control through emotional distortion, mental manipulation, and image management.

Passive perpetrators often position themselves as the misunderstood or martyred figure. They may subtly discredit others while elevating their own moral standing. To outsiders, they appear trustworthy; to those closest to them, the relationship can feel confusing, draining, and disorienting.

The core of a passive controller is often a fragile ego—afraid of exposure, failure, or rejection. Insecurity drives their behavior, and they may be unaware of the harm they cause, as self-preservation overrides self-awareness. For those in relationships with them, the dynamic often feels like being trapped in a fog—constantly second-guessing reality, emotions, and truth.

COMMON TRAITS AND BEHAVIORS OF PASSIVE CONTROLLERS:

- Guilt-tripping or emotionally withdrawing to gain compliance
- Reframing conflict to make themselves the victim
- Refusing to take ownership while subtly shifting blame
- Using "kindness" or helpfulness as a form of leverage
- Publicly affirming others while privately criticizing or undermining
- Gas-lighting—causing others to question their memory, instincts, or feelings
- Playing the role of the misunderstood or spiritual martyr
- Avoiding direct confrontation but manipulating outcomes behind the scenes
- Controlling through charm, piety, or emotional dependence
- Expecting loyalty or emotional caretaking without reciprocation

Still, not all perpetrators act out of arrogance or self-interest. Many are deeply wounded individuals, carrying shame they do not know how to process. They alternate between guilt and image repair, vacillating between their "bad" and "good" selves in an attempt to soothe their internal distress.

Recognizing these dynamics does not excuse abusive behavior—but it does invite compassion, accountability, and the hope of transformation. Healing is possible, but only when perpetrators face the truth of their actions, own the impact they've caused, and are willing to seek real, lasting change.

PERPETRATORS AND BOUNDARIES

Perpetrators often have little regard for the boundaries of others. They feel entitled to take what they want if it benefits their agenda and use manipulation as a means of control. When confronted with wrongdoing, they frequently gaslight their victims, saying things like:

"What's wrong with you?"
"It's just in your head."
"You're too sensitive."

These phrases are designed to shift blame and discredit the reality of the one who challenges them. In many cases, perpetrators will even adopt the role of the victim themselves, flipping the narrative to gain sympathy and avoid responsibility. They twist their position of power into a stance of weakness when it suits their purposes, often waiting for someone to come to their emotional rescue.

To better understand this dynamic, consider an example:

Joe is a verbally abusive husband—an aggressive controller—who lives in a state of emotional volatility. His rage is so intense that Linda, his wife, does everything she can to keep the peace. She walks on eggshells, trying to avoid triggering another outburst. Over time, she internalizes the blame, believing Joe's behavior is somehow her fault. She numbs her pain with alcohol—not just to escape Joe's anger, but to silence old wounds left by her abusive father. As she detaches emotionally, Joe casts himself as the victim. Her drinking becomes evidence of her "failure" in his eyes, while his own behavior remains unquestioned.

Copyright Spirit of Life Recovery. All Rights Reserved.

This story illustrates the fluid nature of dysfunctional systems. Roles shift constantly. The perpetrator becomes the victim. The victim becomes the rescuer. These roles morph based on need and emotion. One person claims the moral high ground while remaining blind to their own behavior. These patterns are not rooted in reality—they are driven by inner wounds, shame, and the need for control.

Joe never faces his behavior. He isn't challenged. Meanwhile, Linda is crushed under the weight of both his accusations and her own pain. She carries her suffering and his. And yet, her pain becomes a catalyst. She begins to awaken to the truth and slowly finds the courage to name the dynamic for what it is. She begins to set boundaries—not out of rebellion, but from a deep desire for healing.

Joe remains stuck in the cycle, protected by the narrative he's built. For perpetrators like him, the primary boundary is this: I must be right. Others must be wrong.

BEING IN A RELATIONSHIP WITH A PERPETRATOR

Whether the abuse is overt or covert, the result is the same: confusion, emotional exhaustion, and a slow erosion of identity. Truth is distorted. Safety is compromised. You may begin to question your memory, your intentions—even your sanity. Conversations circle endlessly. No matter how you try to resolve the issue, it always comes back to you being at fault.

You begin to shrink. You trade your voice for peace. You silence your needs to avoid conflict. Over time, your sense of self weakens. The relationship becomes unbearable. And yet, leaving isn't always the immediate solution. The first step is clarity. Healing begins when you reclaim your truth—when you stop trying to manage the perpetrator and begin restoring your voice. Whether you remain in the relationship or not, freedom begins when you step out of the role they've assigned and into the identity God has given you: whole, loved, and free.

WHAT THE PERPETRATOR NEEDS

Just like the victim, the perpetrator needs healing. But their healing cannot begin without accountability. They cannot be comforted into change—they must be confronted. If no one holds up a mirror, they may never see themselves. When their behavior is tolerated, the pattern deepens.

Behaviors have spiritual roots. Perpetrator behavior often aligns with the demonic realm, seeking to gain power through fear, manipulation, and deception. While we can understand the human pain behind their story, their behavior is not just broken—it is spiritually harmful. This is not something we justify, excuse, or coddle. Perpetrator behavior is abusive, wrong, and sometimes outright evil.

Covert perpetrators—especially those who appear moral or spiritual—are particularly difficult to challenge. But boundaries are essential. The moment someone refuses to be controlled is the moment the perpetrator is forced to face themselves. And that is what they fear most.

Copyright Spirit of Life Recovery. All Rights Reserved.

Perpetrators are not truly strong—they are deeply insecure. Anger and manipulation are their armor. Beneath the surface is a terrified heart. If they relax their grip, they fear being exposed and undone.

Every perpetrator carries a wounded child within. Some never connect with that part of themselves. Others eventually face the truth: something inside is broken. That awareness is sacred. It is the first invitation to healing. No amount of behavior modification will help unless the deeper story is addressed. What's underneath the rage? What's beneath the control? That's where the healing begins.

Perpetrators need grace—and then more grace. They need space to face their truth without shame. And yet, they must be called to account. They are not monsters—they are human beings using destructive strategies to survive.

Still, compassion is never permission. God is both mercy and justice. He holds perpetrators accountable and offers redemption. His love does not ignore harm. Without truth, there is no healing. Without repentance, there is no reconciliation. And without accountability, there is no change.

Perpetrators filled with abuse, neglect, and harmful control are not safe. They do not deserve to be coddled or treated as if they are incapable of change. They can change. But it is their responsibility to seek transformation.

#3. CYCLE OF PAIN: RESCUER

In every painful cycle involving victims and perpetrators, the third role that often emerges is the rescuer. This role may be the most overlooked, often seen as admirable or even godly. And indeed, when we think of a true rescuer, we think of Jesus—our ultimate Savior. He rescues in purity, with power and truth. But many of us, unknowingly, step into a distorted version of that role. We try to rescue not from Spirit-led love, but from brokenness and unconscious need.

Rescuers are often shaped by childhood environments that lacked emotional stability. Raised in chaotic homes, these children quickly learn that if peace is going to exist, they must be the ones to create it. Their desire to help comes from sincere motives, but it develops into a learned pattern: I must take responsibility for everyone else's emotions in order to feel safe.

As these children grow into adults, they are often admired for their strength, reliability, and competence. They are deeply empathetic, naturally inclined to step in when others are in crisis. But beneath this outward strength lies a silent struggle. They carry emotional weight that was never theirs to bear. They have unmet needs that they've buried under layers of external caretaking. Over time, their helpfulness becomes compulsive. They enter relationships not just to love, but to fix. And slowly, they begin to lose themselves.

Consider Sophie's story. Raised in a home filled with conflict, she often mediated arguments between her parents. Her efforts were praised, even used as leverage by her parents to validate their own points. In trying to keep peace, Sophie learned to disconnect from her own needs. Instead of being parented, she parented her parents. When they divorced, she internalized their failure as her own. Her life became a quest to do better, fix more, be enough. Her childhood formed a rescuer identity so deeply ingrained, it followed her into every adult relationship. And like Sophie, many rescuers are exhausted, fragmented, and still trying to earn the love they never received.

THE RESCUER IN RELATIONSHIP

Rescuers tend to enter into codependent relationships, where their worth is measured by how much they give. Their emotional compass is set to other people's feelings. They become entangled, enmeshed, and overwhelmed. Though they may appear competent on the outside, they are often struggling to keep themselves together internally.

Their relationships are imbalanced. They give endlessly and receive little. They take on the role of the caretaker, the planner, the one who always shows up. But under this strength is often a buildup of resentment and loneliness. They feel unappreciated, unseen, and yet unable to stop rescuing. They are caught in a loop that feeds on their need to be needed.

Rescuers often believe they are doing the loving thing, but in reality, they may be enabling dysfunction. By rescuing someone from the consequences of their behavior, they prevent them from growing. They carry responsibilities that aren't theirs. They step in, take over, smooth things out, and call it peace—but it's not real peace. It's avoidance.

Sometimes, rescuers even minimize the behavior of perpetrators by offering sympathy instead of boundaries. For example, a parent of an addicted adult child may make excuses for their behavior, shielding them from consequences. Their compassion, while sincere, becomes a barrier to healing. They try to fix what only God can.

Let's look at a more detailed example:

Jill shows up drunk to a family reunion, cursing, demeaning others, and eventually slapping her aunt in a fit of rage. Her parents rush to her side, trying to comfort and excuse her behavior. They explain away her actions, even applauding her for "protecting" her sister from past abuse. They apologize to everyone involved but never address the root issue. No one is held accountable. The real pain is avoided. Everyone stays stuck. Jill continues to self-destruct, her aunt's wounds remain buried, and the parents maintain the illusion of peace.

This is the rescuer dynamic in action. Pain is never dealt with—just managed. The rescuer is not healing; they are maintaining dysfunction.

RESCUERS AND BOUNDARIES

Rescuers struggle deeply with boundaries. They enter spaces uninvited. They take on responsibilities no one asked them to take. They make decisions for others under the guise of love. They do for others what others should be doing for themselves.

They don't hold people accountable. They buffer the consequences of poor choices. They turn harmful behavior into a need for more care. This might feel like compassion, but it disables others. It prevents victims from stepping into their own power and healing. Rescuers often confuse enabling with love.

At times, rescuers even reinterpret a perpetrator's harmful actions through a sympathetic lens, distorting the truth. In doing so, they become complicit. They may believe they're bringing peace, but they are sustaining chaos. If you confront them, they may become defensive, unable to see the part they play in perpetuating dysfunction. They truly believe they are the glue holding everything together.

Common Attributes of the Rescuer Identity:

- Emotionally disconnected from self, over-attuned to others' emotions
- Gains identity through helping others
- Avoids personal needs and inner work
- Over-functions in relationships
- Becomes the enabler of dysfunction
- Maintains false peace at the expense of truth
- Feels needed but rarely feels seen
- Easily shifts into resentment or burnout
- Needs crisis to maintain relevance

WHAT RESCUERS NEED

Rescuers often believe that needing help is a weakness. They may even feel ashamed to have needs at all. Their sense of worth has become tied to their usefulness. But beneath that over-functioning is a wounded heart—one that longs to be loved not for what it does, but for who it is.

The turning point for many rescuers comes in crisis. When they finally break under the weight of what they've been carrying, they are faced with their own limitations. This breaking can become a breakthrough. It is in that moment that they have a chance to turn toward the only One who can truly rescue them: Jesus.

Of all the roles, the rescuer may be the one that most easily masquerades as Christlike. It looks holy. It feels noble. But when it comes from wounding, it keeps people trapped. Jesus doesn't just save— He restores. He doesn't enable dysfunction—He transforms it. When He becomes the rescuer for the rescuer, the healing begins.

Rescuers need to be seen. They need to be comforted. They need someone to say, "You don't have to carry it all." They need grace to untangle their worth from their works. They need permission to lay it down.

And most of all, they need to know this: their needs matter too. Their healing matters. Their heart matters. Underneath the rescuer identity is often a forgotten victim, a neglected child who never got to receive. That part must be brought into the light, named, and nurtured. And only grace can do that.

HOW GOD HEALS THE RESCUER

God doesn't just call rescuers to stop helping. He calls them to receive help. He gently invites them out of self-reliance and into holy dependence. He teaches them that love is not performance. Worth is not earned.

Through Jesus, rescuers are reminded that they are not the Savior—He is. And He is good. He doesn't demand burnout. He doesn't reward martyrdom. He invites healing. He fills empty places. He lifts burdens. And He teaches them a new way: not to rescue, but to love with wisdom, boundaries, and Spirit-led compassion.

When rescuers begin to live from a place of being loved instead of needing to be needed, they become truly free. And in that freedom, they no longer keep others weak—they empower them to grow.

This is the redemption of the rescuer: to receive what they never had, to become whole, and to help from a place of healing instead of a place of lack.

Because only when we let God rescue us can we be part of someone else's healing story without becoming the story ourselves.

STEPPING OUT OF THE CYCLE

These roles—victim, perpetrator, and rescuer—are not our true identity. They are the masks we wear, the habits we form, and the roles we adopt to navigate a broken world. They are our attempts to survive trauma, make sense of pain, and feel in control.

The question is: Are we ready to release these faulty roles? Do we want to break these cycles? Do we want to learn to defend ourselves with boundaries in a more productive way? Before we can break into a new pattern, we need to define the pattern of "what is." Assessment work is never the final stop—it is the first act of courage. Not from guilt or shame, but from awareness and grace.

The roles we've explored are familiar because they resemble what we experience through our relationships, our thoughts, and our coping mechanisms. But they are not our destination. We were not created to live as victims, perpetrators, or rescuers. We were created to be free in our identity in Christ.

Approach this process like a detective. Follow the trail of emotions, reactions, and relational patterns. Ask the hard questions: Where did I learn this? Why do I respond this way? What am I trying to protect? Seek not condemnation, but clarity. Not perfection, but progress.

And as you do, remember this: You are not alone. God walks with you through every layer of this work. His Spirit reveals truth not to shame you, but to free you. He is your healer, your defender, and your guide. And He is faithful to complete the work He begins in you.

Application:
Worksheet "Victim, Perpetrator and Rescuer" (Page 20)

VICTIM, PERPETRATOR AND RESCUER IDENTIFICATION WORKSHEET

In my relationship with (name the person)
_____

I am victim when
_____
_____
_____

I am a perpetrator when
_____
_____
_____

I am a rescuer when
_____
_____
_____

They victimize me when
_____
_____
_____

They try to save me when
_____
_____
_____

They make me the perpetrator when
_____
_____
_____

Can you identify your primary role? How do you switch to other roles? Why?
_____
_____
_____
_____

Copyright Spirit of Life Recovery. All Rights Reserved.

PART 2
Grace & Shame

The cycles of pain we operate in—whether as victim, perpetrator, or rescuer—are rooted in powerlessness. In these roles, we often use subtle or overt forms of control in an attempt to make others behave the way we want or to meet needs that were left unmet in our own lives. We rarely do this consciously. Most of us don't know any other way to survive. This subconscious striving, often born from an "orphan mentality," leaves us chasing fulfillment in ways that continue the very cycles we want to escape.

But healing does not begin with escape. The starting point isn't to run away and work on ourselves in isolation. It begins by surrendering the illusion that we can change or fix anyone. This moment of realization can feel disorienting—even defeating. It feels like loss. It feels like weakness.

But this space of powerlessness isn't failure—it's sacred. It's the very gateway into the deeper mystery of transformation. This is where we discover the power of God—not just as a concept, but as the very substance we were made to run on.

God's power is unlike any earthly force. It shows up in the form of love, value, and acceptance. It gives us the ability to live loved—and living loved births true freedom. When we live from this place, we don't need to enforce boundaries out of fear—we draw them out of love. They become expressions of internal wholeness rather than defenses against pain.

Imagine the Father in Heaven operating out of fear or insecurity. It's impossible. He is perfectly stable and confident because He knows who He is. His agenda is settled. We, on the other hand, often lack that same internal certainty. We compromise our value for temporary needs. We exchange truth for approval. We make ourselves small so we can feel safe.

This is why we need a power greater than intellect or human willpower. We need the power of love—true love—as a transformative force. We need it not only to heal but to reshape how we see and carry ourselves in this world.

THE INNER WORK OF TRANSFORMATION

This journey of accessing God's love and reclaiming our value is not simply theological—it is deeply personal. It must be imprinted on our soul. It must seep into our being and heal us from the inside out. It must expose and replace the false roles we've taken on.

If we try to form new behaviors or structures from the outside in, we only reinforce the same cycles that wounded us. Our deepest needs are internal—and the solution must begin there.

Copyright Spirit of Life Recovery. All Rights Reserved.

This doesn't mean we ignore unhealthy relational patterns or avoid new communication tools. It doesn't mean we pretend the pain isn't real. It means we acknowledge that before we can build new habits or boundaries, we must first possess the power to do so. That power doesn't come from others. It's not found in books or strategies alone. It must be contained in our own hearts—planted by grace and sustained by the Spirit.

Admittedly, this can be frustrating to hear—especially when the pain we feel is caused by others. It seems unfair to carry the weight of change when we are not the ones who hurt others. But the truth is this: just as a drained battery cannot function until it's charged, our hearts cannot operate in health without a new internal power structure.

And so the question becomes: how do we access that power?

THE ACTUAL THREAT

There are two forces of power constantly waging war within us, and many of us are fighting a battle we don't even realize we're in. Shame and grace are both seeking to gain access to our hearts and minds. While it may sound dramatic to frame our internal struggles in such terms, this perspective gives us critical insight into why we need Christ in our lives. If we lack spiritual resources to sustain us through life's breakdowns, what, then, is the purpose of our faith?

Psychological principles can help us understand our humanity, but only spiritual truths can identify and uproot the deeper culprits. And the remarkable part is this: accessing the cure is not as hard as it seems. But before we receive it, we must understand the battleground.

In the cycles of pain, we are not ultimately fighting people—we are fighting the shame that infects people. Like an invisible virus, shame works subtly, without detection, yet with devastating impact. It is the wrecking ball that shatters lives, relationships, and families. Shame is the awful feeling of never measuring up. It makes us feel dirty, rejected, and unworthy. And its greatest power lies in its ability to remain hidden.

Shame tells us we are unlovable, unseen, defective, and unfixable. It marks our inner world with unworthiness and enslaves us to its message. It's what keeps us in bondage.

Shame becomes systemic. It overtakes our thoughts, drives our emotions, and is even imprinted in our brains. It influences our bodies, our health, and our behavior—driving everything from depression to addiction. Yet at its core, shame is not just emotional or psychological—it's spiritual. It is the residue of the fall, the force that first caused Adam and Eve to hide from God in the garden.

The brutality of shame lies in what it severs. It disconnects us from God, causing us to hide or rebel. It disconnects us from ourselves, forging a false identity. It disconnects us from others, creating distance and dysfunction in relationships. At the root of shame is rejection—a deep fear of not being enough, of being unworthy of love, safety, or belonging.

Copyright Spirit of Life Recovery. All Rights Reserved.

When left unhealed, shame multiplies through layers of pain, betrayal, and abandonment, reinforcing its toxic narrative. And because it operates in secrecy, we often fail to recognize it for what it is.

Naming shame as the enemy gives us clarity. It allows us to separate the presence of shame from our personal identity—and from the identity of others. In other words, we are not the shame we feel. Neither are those who project their shame onto us. Once we see this clearly, we can begin to manage shame, set boundaries, and pursue healing.

However, this is often where we get stuck. Even when we recognize shame's grip, the solution can feel vague or out of reach. Confronting shame requires vulnerability—a risk not everyone feels ready to take. And knowledge alone is not enough to free us.

To overcome shame, we must access a superior source of power—one strong enough to consume shame at its roots. That power is grace.

FINDING POWER

Grace, like shame, is hard to define. It is invisible. But its impact is the exact opposite of shame. Where shame wounds, grace restores. Where shame rejects, grace accepts. Where shame says, "You are unworthy," grace declares, "You are more than enough."

So why would anyone reject grace? Because we misunderstand it. We often think of grace as leniency or a divine loophole—a "get out of jail free" card. Some have been taught that grace is weak, indulgent, or permissive. Others believe it's just religious language for ignoring sin. But real grace is none of these things.

Grace is the power of Father God's redemption plan. It is His divine influence flowing from the cross. Jesus was sent to carry grace. He bore the full weight of shame—the dirt, rejection, and brokenness—and took it onto Himself. As a transaction, grace paid the debt of shame. It consumed its force completely.

Jesus is the true Rescuer. When hell's forces came to destroy us with weapons of shame, Jesus stood in our place and took the hit. He bore the wound of shame's destruction. And because Jesus overcame shame, the power He now offers us is greater.

Where sin and shame once ruled, grace now reigns. If shame and grace were placed in a ring, grace would win every time.

Grace says, "You are accepted, seen, known, and worthy"—not because of what you've done, but because of who God says you are. But grace requires one thing: unworthiness. That's right. Grace is not earned through merit. It is received only when we admit we don't deserve it. That is the radical and beautiful paradox of the gospel. We don't become worthy to get grace. Grace makes us worthy.

This is our hope. This is our way out of shame. And this is the real power that transforms us from the inside out.

MISUNDERSTANDING GRACE

More often than not, we miss out on the redemptive attributes of grace. We say, "I'm going to heaven—grace saved me from death," and then live out the rest of our lives powerless and defeated. Grace becomes a one-time transaction, and we continue living from the fruit of shame and the cycles and patterns it produces, all while claiming we are under grace. This is utterly confusing. It causes us to live not only powerless in our relational connections but powerless in our Christian journey.

Inserting Christianity into a shame-based framework is a crisis. That's because grace is the power we need to break cycles and find freedom. Shame only reminds us of our failures and our perceived ineligibility before God. As a result, shame causes us to flee God's protection or to act from a place of self-righteousness. Grace, on the other hand, draws us to God and awakens us to our dependency on Him.

To bring grace into our hearts, we must allow it to enter us in a way that transforms us from the inside out. The world has conformed us, as Romans 12:2 says, through its ideas about us. People have influenced us with their interpretations of who we are. But Jesus comes to renew us and transform us into His idea, His image. And that isn't a behavioral obligation—it's a power source. In other words, God doesn't hand us a list of how we need to change and expect us to carry it out on our own. Instead, He gives us the actual power to change.

So, if this is true and real, why do we live our lives as though it never happened?

It is astounding to realize how often we deny this power when we reduce the Christian life to a set of standards. If we measure our Christian journey by what we do, how we do it, or how morally we behave, we are by default living under the system of shame. Shame applauds our efforts when we measure up, which subtly becomes pride. And it just as quickly condemns us when we fail or fall short of the standard, causing us to self-reject and loathe. In either case, shame is an inward attachment to our own effort, and that is the very opposite of what grace does in us.

It's not that grace condones sin or darkness—it certainly doesn't. But it is by no means afraid of or offended by it. Grace has an appetite for what's wrong and damaged, in order to make it right. Living by grace means bringing our brokenness to God and asking for help. This is a principle Paul discusses in Romans 7.

We don't get grace by doing. We don't earn it through our titles or tithes. We can't be enough or not enough for it. Grace establishes the ultimate standard—it is the level playing field where we become enough simply because our names are written in the Lamb's Book of Life. We are enough because we bear the title Child of the Living God, and we are loved with an everlasting love. This presentation of our brokenness to Heaven stands in contrast to the presentation of our good deeds.

People reject grace in many ways. Some believe God only wants them if they're good. Others reject it because they don't think they are good enough. Still, others reject grace because they want to maintain their personal power. And so, whatever human power they have managed to gain—that will be all they ever have.

But if we surrender that personal power—if we let the walls of our secrets and hiding be exposed before the eternal God—if we allow ourselves to be weak and unable in His presence, this is where grace is received.

Each time He said, "My grace is all you need. My power works best in weakness." So now I am glad to boast about my weaknesses, so that the power of Christ can work through me. That's why I take pleasure in my weaknesses, and in the insults, hardships, persecutions, and troubles that I suffer for Christ. For when I am weak, then I am strong. (2 Corinthians 12:9–10)

The word "power" in this verse comes from the Greek word *dunamis*, which refers to God's supernatural ability. It is the power of God to do for us what we cannot do for ourselves. This is the very ingredient and essence of grace. Grace was activated at the cross and becomes the very function of our life in Him. We walk in grace. It is the resource we need for life. Grace is power. And apparently, it is accessed through our weakness.

The word "weakness" comes from the Greek word *asthéneia*. According to HELPS Word-Studies, it refers to an ailment that deprives someone of enjoying or accomplishing. We must grasp the incredible irony of Jesus saying, "My power works best in weakness." In other words, God's power begins where our power ends. It may not sound romantic—rather, it sounds messy. But like a bed of dirt, when we allow God to plant grace in our hearts, it will take root and prosper in the middle of the mess.

LEAVING POWERLESSNESS

Leaving the powerlessness of the cycles of pain for grace through Jesus requires surrender and a mindset change. Surrender is perhaps the hardest part. If you are hungry for real change, the first step is simply admitting the powerlessness you carry. It really is that simple. But applying that power to our real life takes time. Some of us may have dramatic breakthroughs, but those don't even bring lasting change. Real change is rooted, much like a tree that is planted and grows, and thus we cannot put pressure on ourselves to immediately retain a new state of mind.

Grace is the glue that holds our life together and sustains us in the places where we don't have our act together. That's one of the many superpowers it contains. Since it is the grand provider of what we need and ascribes our worth to us, it doesn't even matter what our life looks like. We begin as we are. We start in the exact form we are in. We don't try to get fit in order to be worthy for the gym; we use the gym to gain fitness. In the same manner, we don't get right to receive grace. We use grace to birth the transformation and change we desire. Grace is as competent to perform on our behalf as the power of shame was capable of birthing pain and brokenness.

Learning to walk into a new mindset and leave our victim, perpetrator, and rescuer cycles behind us will not come easy or naturally at first. It's like moving against a current—we just don't have

Copyright Spirit of Life Recovery. All Rights Reserved.

the strength to do it. But when we can admit that we are weak, we can ask God to be strong on our behalf.

The power statements we refer to throughout the remainder of this material are a way of responding to our current mindsets with a truth about God's love and His power. We can't deny that we believe or act out in certain ways. If we perceive our wrongness or failure as a defining feature of our identity, we will begin to drown in shame's influence.

Honesty is the opposite of shame. Shame attempts to be discreet and hide. Honesty calls it out and admits it is present. Once we expose the shame, we can present it with an appropriate response. A power statement is no small thing. If you choose to believe it, it will transform you within. A power statement says something like this:

Even though I am _____ (name something that makes you feel bad about yourself), I am loved, valued, and accepted by God.

Shame already made power statements in our life, and we should never underestimate their force. They said things like:

- You'll never be good enough, so stop trying
- No one can love you because something is wrong with you
- You will be rejected if people know who you are
- You will fail because you always fail
- You are only valuable by what you do
- You always mess up

When God makes claims for our life, they are real. The power of them is activated when we agree with them.

- You are inherently worthy, valued, and loved
- You are precious
- You are honored
- You are respected
- You are defined by worthiness
- You are the cost of grace

Coming into agreement with grace grants us authority over shame. What does this mean? If we grab onto the truth of a power statement, it can crush and weed out the shame. Maybe it won't root immediately, but if that truth can replace the power of the shame, it will ferociously change our heart.

Power statements, if anything, are reminders that we have power. We are not weak. We are not defenseless. We can change. We can overcome. We can find a better way. They don't hold supernatural power in word alone, but in the ability to construct long-term mindsets that align with God's truth.

Power statements aren't necessarily a miraculous and momentous shift in the moment. But like building a new track inside our heart, we start giving our heart and even our brain a new pathway to believe and operate from. In some ways, you could say we are developing a new "exit plan" to manage the difficulties in life. The old exit plans are the cycles of pain. The new ones are the stabilizing truth of the power statement.

APPLYING POWER STATEMENTS TO END THE CYCLES

Each role in the cycle of pain—victim, perpetrator, rescuer—engages with shame in a different way. Understanding how shame functions within each role allows us to respond with the right kind of power statement. Awareness becomes our first step in transformation. Shame may try to dominate our hearts, but it does not get the final say unless we give it permission.

While this section focuses on the role of shame, later content will go deeper into boundaries and practical tools. For now, let's focus on identifying how shame plays out in our specific cycle and craft power statements accordingly.

VICTIMS ABSORB SHAME

Victims often give shame—and the people who speak it—great power and credibility. They take on the messages of shame as absolute truth. This leads to a deep feeling of powerlessness and an internal belief that change is not possible. Victims may even begin to feel morally superior to others, falling into a "better than" or "less than" mentality. This, too, is a form of shame.

A power statement captures the false messages and replaces them with God's affirmation. Victims need voices of help, affirmation, and guidance to outweigh the pain or violation they've experienced. When a victim receives a power statement, they are choosing to let God's voice have authority over the voices of their pain.

Power Statement for Victims:
Even if _____ (name a person) _____ (name a behavior), I am loved, valued, and accepted by God. I am who God says I am. I don't have to live under shame's message. Therefore, I have choices to change _____.

PERPETRATORS IMPUTE SHAME

Perpetrators often express shame outwardly—through control, criticism, or aggression. They pass on shame in words and behaviors. Some do this unknowingly. Others, more deeply wounded or hardened, do it from a place of severe brokenness. Regardless of intent, the force of shame is real and damaging.

Recognizing these behaviors is the first step to healing. Grace may call us to make amends in time, but the initial step is to receive it. A power statement doesn't justify harmful behavior—it begins the process of stopping it. These statements soften the heart, awaken humility, and open the door to transformation.

Power Statement for Perpetrators:
Even if I _____ (name a behavior) against _____ (name a person), I am loved, valued, and accepted by God. Therefore, I have the power to stop my wrongdoing and cease control.

RESCUERS MANAGE SHAME

Rescuers try to carry everyone's burdens—including their shame. They often see themselves as the only solution, taking on the emotional and spiritual weight of others, especially those caught in destructive or abusive patterns. This is exhausting, unsustainable, and spiritually misaligned.

Rescuers must remember: Jesus is the real Healer. We were never meant to be anyone's Savior.

Power Statement for Rescuers:
Even if I rescue _____ (name a person), I am loved, valued, and accepted by God. Therefore, I can trust Jesus to be the real Rescuer.

IN SUMMARY

Power statements don't change others, but they create a net—a boundary—that catches shame before it embeds itself again. Shame's power lies in its message. Power statements give us a new message—one from God.

They may feel foreign at first. You might speak them without emotion or belief. But over time, if you hold onto them like seeds and water them with truth, they will grow. They will take root in your soul. And they will become the new foundation from which you live.

Worksheets
Chart: Understanding Shame Cycles (Page 29)
Worksheet: Power Statements for Each Role (Page 30)
Comparison: Shame vs. Grace Worksheet (Page 31)

STOPPING SHAME CYCLES

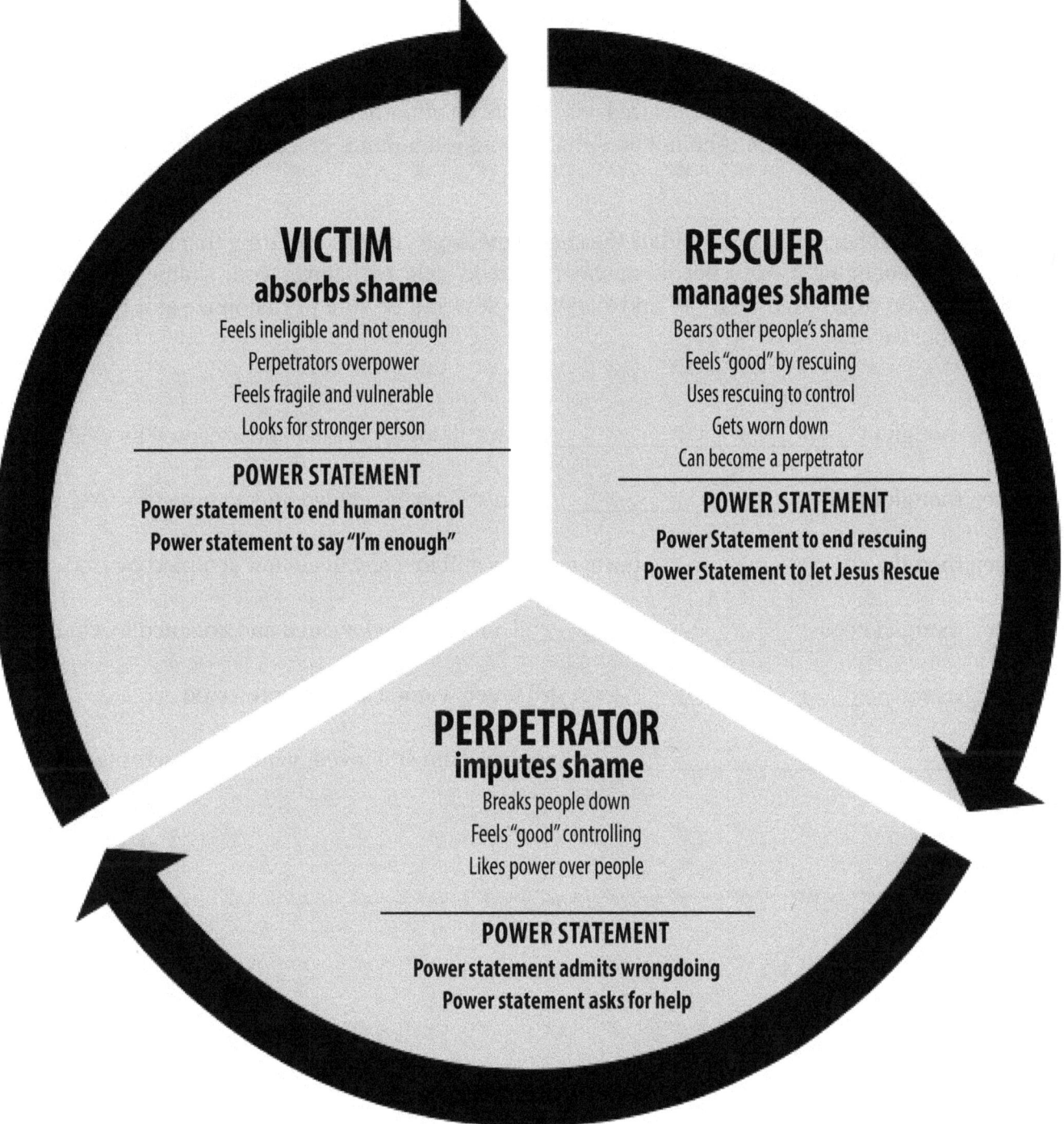

POWER STATEMENTS

This week, learn to practice the awareness and recognition of shame messages. Instead of judging yourself negative, think of it more in terms of finding clues and solving a mystery. You are on the "hunt" to discover how much shame is lodged in your day to day life. When you discover shame, imagine you are going to trap shame in a box, and then "feed" it a power statement.

It might seem silly at a surface level, but its an attempt to train the inner system that shame isn't normal or true. And not only that, it begins announce grace as a higher and more potent resource.

Remember, when you validate the shame message you are admitting that it exists, but you are challenging it. Your power statement should reflect whatever your shame message was that you discovered. You can find example below, but be sure to customize and learn to write your own.

Even though I _____, I am still loved, valued and accepted by God.

Even though I feel _____, I am still loved, valued and accepted by God.

Even though _____ hurts me, I am still loved, valued and accepted by God.

Even though I need _____, I am still loved, valued and accepted by God.

Even if I am _____, I am still loved, valued and accepted God.

Even if _____ happens, I am still loved, valued and accepted by God.

SHAME & GRACE

How we walk into shame represents the general way we see the world. If we live under the domination of shame, it has power in our life. But just the same, if we become marked by grace, we can have those fundamental mindsets changed. The system we carry is what we offer. We see people through the same filter we see ourselves. This is why shame is so catastrophic in relationships.

SHAME SPEAKS TO ME	GRACE SPEAKS TO ME
I failed	I did my best
Something is wrong with me	I'm okay
I deserve punishment	I need another chance
I'm not enough	I'm worthy
I have so many faults	I am a work in progress
No one meets my needs	God meets my needs
I am what I do	I am who God says
I never do it right	I give what I have
I'll never change	I change with grace

OTHERS SHAME ME	OTHERS GIVE ME GRACE
You failed me	You did your best
Something is wrong with you	You're okay
You deserve punishment	You can have another chance
You have so many faults	You are a work in progress
You don't meet my needs	You give what you have
You are what you do	You are who God says
You never do right	You give what you have
You'll never change	You change with grace

How do you offer shame and grace in your relationships? How do you receive shame and grace?

_____
_____
_____
_____
_____
_____
_____
_____
_____

Copyright Spirit of Life Recovery. All Rights Reserved.

PART 3
Healing Cycles of Pain

Relationships caught in cycles of pain often operate through a false sense of connection. A crisis, unmet need, or trauma response becomes the foundation of the bond, and over time, dysfunction begins to feel normal. These patterns are often mistaken for closeness, even love. But what feels like connection is actually survival—and survival is not the same as safety. This creates an unhealthy bond where distorted roles and relational patterns are confused with affection, closeness, or passion. The chaos becomes familiar. Familiarity begins to feel like love, but it's not love—it's pain that has been normalized.

In a healthy relationship, bonding happens when mutual needs are acknowledged, valued, and communicated. Each person cares for the needs of the other—not out of fear or obligation, but from a place of freedom. Over time, trust is built as needs are expressed, respected, and met. In this kind of relationship, love binds hearts together through gentleness, kindness, and care.

In a trauma bond, dysfunction is confused with intimacy. The emotional highs and lows—withdrawal and reconciliation, shame and rescue—are interpreted as passion or intensity. Sometimes even abuse becomes a strange form of bonding. But this isn't connection—it's captivity. And captivity that feels familiar is often mistaken for love.

These bonds are deeply rooted in cycles of pain:

- The victim feels seen in their suffering and believes they don't deserve better.
- The perpetrator seeks power or control, often repeating their own unhealed trauma.
- The rescuer feels responsible for keeping the relationship together, often at great personal cost.

Each role may meet a psychological need, but not a healthy one. These identities create structure in chaos, but they are counterfeit. They keep people locked in a system that feeds on shame and fear.

The tragedy of trauma bonds is that healing often feels threatening. Becoming well means stepping out of the role you've used to survive. And when one person steps out, the system begins to collapse. Without the cycle of victim, perpetrator, and rescuer, there is no more scaffolding. For many, that loss feels terrifying. But in truth, what collapses is not love—it's dysfunction. And what rises in its place is the invitation to real connection, rooted not in fear or survival, but in truth and freedom.

THE CYCLE OF A TRAUMA BOND

While trauma bonds may vary in form, most follow a similar repetitive cycle:

Idealization – One person (often the perpetrator or rescuer) creates a sense of safety, attention, or affection that feels like genuine love or connection. The bond intensifies quickly.

Tension – Shame, unmet needs, and emotional triggers build beneath the surface. Something begins to feel off, but no one acknowledges it.

Devaluation – Conflict or emotional harm occurs. The victim feels responsible or worthless. The perpetrator may shame or blame. The rescuer attempts to fix or appease.

Reconciliation – Apologies, promises, or emotional connection resurface. There may be a "honeymoon phase" or spiritual justification for continuing. Hope is rekindled.

Repeat – The cycle begins again, reinforcing the bond and entrenching the roles.

Over time, each loop of this cycle further entangles the individuals. Their roles solidify. The pain feels normal. The bond, though toxic, feels necessary—sometimes even sacred.

WHY THE CYCLE MUST BE BROKEN

When one person in the trauma bond begins to heal and step out of their role, the system can no longer function as it once did. The cycle dissolves. This can feel terrifying to everyone involved, especially if the relationship was the primary source of identity, purpose, or belonging.

But this unraveling is also the invitation to something real—to love that is rooted in truth, not pain.

Healing begins with this awareness: you are not your role. You are not the victim, the perpetrator, or the rescuer. You may have played those parts to survive, but they are not your identity.

Grace offers us a new path—a path that acknowledges the pain but does not define us by it. It empowers us to step out of the shame system and live from the truth of who God says we are.

This transformation cannot be forced on others, and that's one of the hardest realities to accept. But it can start with you. You can begin to heal your side of the relational pattern by bringing grace into your own internal system. You can break the cycle—not by changing others—but by changing what you agree with inside yourself.

When you begin to live loved, to live valued, and to live free, you will naturally change the way you relate to others. You'll gain clarity on what kind of relationship is worth building—and what boundaries must be drawn to protect your healing.

THE GRACE TO HEAL THE PAST

There are two essential kinds of healing every person needs: healing from the past and healing in the present. While current challenges often require boundaries, conflict resolution, and relational tools—topics we'll explore in the chapters ahead—healing from the past asks something deeper. It calls us inward. It calls us to remember.

Past healing is a process of uncovering where shame took root. These roots often lie buried in places where hurt was never properly processed, where grief was never validated, or where no one helped us make sense of our pain. Not every wound becomes a stronghold—but the ones that did were often those we walked through alone.

The goal is not to dig up everything that ever hurt us. The goal is to become aware of the unresolved places still influencing our present. These hidden roots shape how we see ourselves, how we react in relationships, and how we cope under pressure. They can even cause us to project past experiences into present ones—not because the threat is real, but because the pain still is.

We carry unhealed versions of ourselves into relationships, hoping someone or something will finally make it right. But instead of moving beyond the wound, we often reinforce it. The cycle of pain continues—new faces, familiar outcomes.

To begin healing, we must first recognize the roles we've played within those cycles—roles we took on to survive: the victim, the perpetrator, and the rescuer. These are not our true identities. They are coping mechanisms, shaped by unmet needs and broken places. The goal is not to wear them as labels—but to see them clearly enough to be set free.

HEALING THE VICTIM ROOTS

Among the three roles, most of us carry some part of the victim within. This identity is deeply intertwined with shame. To understand this more fully, we need to see how shame embeds itself in the soul.

Shame takes root through three core beliefs:

"Something is wrong with me. I'm not good enough."

"I don't deserve to be loved or treated right."

"I am bad because of what I've done."

Shame doesn't just affect how we feel—it affects how we see. It distorts our identity. It convinces us we are unworthy of good things. It becomes a prison: one of self-condemnation, self-protection, and eventually self-sabotage. And over time, we begin to expect others to treat us through the same lens with which we view ourselves.

But this is not the heart of God. God's agenda is to restore us—not as more polished versions of our shame-covered selves, but as the deeply loved, whole, and worthy people He created us to be. His love isn't earned—it's freely given. His acceptance isn't conditional—it's an "even if" love; a "no matter what" covenant love. So how do we begin the process of challenging shame's grip? We start by exposing it.

BRINGING SHAME INTO THE LIGHT

If shame hides in victimization, that is the exact place we need to expose. Telling our pain story can begin to remove the power of shame, while also allowing us to release the weight of holding onto pain. When we stuff pain into a box, it doesn't diminish—it builds pressure inside of us and can eventually cause us to implode. This is what Jesus is after: the ability to settle our hearts and gently rewire the painful places with the resources of His power and His grace. Our pain story is sacred ground. It is holy space. It represents the tears and burdens we have carried that Jesus now wants to carry for us. Just as the woman in the Bible wiped her tears with Jesus as she healed, when we offer and present our case to Him, we create an atmosphere that is deeply honoring and pleasing to Him. We let Him into our hearts.

If you have never told your story before, that may be the place to begin. The key is to bring Jesus into your story. Let Him be the Waymaker, moving through the memories of the past and touching them with His power. On a practical level, telling your story needs to be done in a private and safe environment. It should never be shared with someone who might use it against you or exploit your vulnerability. Whether it's a recovery sponsor, mentor, trusted friend, or counselor, these are the safe people to consider. Speaking your pain helps break the power of secrecy. Telling your story is like mapping out the places where pain left its mark—where wounds were created, violations occurred, expectations were unmet, or where we, in turn, hurt others. These become the shaping points of our pain and the survival patterns we developed to cope. When resolution and validation were missing during those moments, we defaulted to self-protection. Recalling those events now allows us to return with something we didn't have then—empathy and validation.

To make it more tangible, imagine being in a devastating car crash, your body crushed inside twisted metal and glass. As you try to escape, you're aware of the internal and external injuries. Now imagine someone showing up and telling you to just get up and move on—without offering help or care. It sounds absurd, yet that is how many of us were treated when we were emotionally or spiritually wounded. We were expected to walk away from deep injuries without aid.

But healing the heart is just like healing the body. We need ointment and care before we can move forward. This may be one of the most misunderstood teachings in Christianity: the idea that we should "forget the past." The truth is, we can't forget the past. It's not buried—it's planted. It's still alive within us, bringing messages from then into now.

TRAUMA AND TRIGGERS

When it comes to trauma and triggers, recalling memories isn't just about reviewing historical facts. It's about facing the emotions that were wounded. When pain went unprocessed, fear and shame became embedded. Fear teaches our body, soul, and spirit what to avoid, and it can develop into irrational responses. A trigger is simply a reaction to a past wound being touched by present circumstances. Anyone with trauma has experienced this. Though trauma often needs deeper care, we can begin to soothe it by understanding that shame and the events that created it are the real enemies. With grace, we gain power over darkness. This doesn't mean we go back and relive the event. But it does mean we retrieve the emotions, validate them, and apply the resources we didn't have at the time.

POWER STATEMENTS IN OUR STORIES

The way Jesus meets you in your pain is unique to your story. We all have different histories, and the same Jesus interacts with each of us differently, showing us what we need to see. That part of healing can't be documented—it's reserved just for you and Him. What we can do, however, is create a power statement from within that memory.

Even though _____ did _____,
I am still loved, valued, and accepted by Jesus.

Even though _____ (name the event),
I am still loved, valued, and accepted by Jesus.

You don't need to believe it fully for it to be powerful. You only need to want it to be true. You can even say "what if" this could be true? The Bible says even the size of a mustard seed—moves mountains.

What gives a power statement its strength isn't just the words—it's the power attached. Grace is not an idea. Grace is a Person.

And when the truth feels far away, you can simply pray:

Jesus, help me. I can't do this without You. I need You.

That's where healing begins. Not in perfection, but in surrender.

HEALING FROM SHAME WHEN WE WERE "NOT ENOUGH"

Once we begin to chart our pain map, we start to see where emotional and relational cycles were formed. Often, our stories reveal key moments where we felt "not good enough." These experiences are typically grounded in shame—the internal sense that we failed to meet a standard or expectation. But here's the catch: shame doesn't always stem from clear rules. The "standard" often shifts depending on the relationship, which is what makes shame so elusive and confusing.

In one family, the expectation might be rigid religious performance without grace. In another, it might be chaos, criminal behavior, or emotional neglect. Because the standard is defined by whoever holds power, we often end up internalizing shame based on someone else's ideals. In essence, we are judged—and judge ourselves—not by truth, but by broken expectations.

To be clear, standards are not inherently bad. Even God's law provides a framework for how to live in wholeness. But when standards are not rooted in truth and love, they create confusion and foster shame. That's why Jesus didn't come to eliminate the law—He came to fulfill it through grace. Where we fall short, He stands in the gap. He doesn't demand perfection; He invites us into transformation through love. When love becomes our motivator, not fear, we can begin to change in safe and lasting ways (see Hebrews 10).

Copyright Spirit of Life Recovery. All Rights Reserved.

In contrast, relationships built on shame feel like emotional prisons. Expectations are used to control. Fear and guilt become motivators. Authenticity gets buried under pressure to perform, and rejection lies at the core. In these dynamics, we aren't free to be ourselves—we're just trying to survive.

Healing invites us to return to those messages of unworthiness and examine the expectations that shaped us. We can do this one relationship at a time—mapping a timeline of where and how "not enough" was communicated. And because shame often speaks through silence or subtle rejection, we need God's help to identify the deeper roots. The Holy Spirit gently reveals how old expectations still influence us today.

This is where grace begins its work. Grace doesn't wait for us to be perfect. It resets the foundation by declaring: "Even if you failed, even if you're still healing, you are still enough. You are still loved. You are still accepted." To be free from shame, we need to do more than recognize the lie—we must receive the truth.

It's incredible how much power other people's expectations can hold over us. But we don't have to stay stuck. Through grace, we can choose a different story—one written by God, not shame.

HEALING THE SHAME OF VIOLATIONS

In addition to expectations driving shame, shame is also deposited in us when people have violated us and assaulted our sense of worth and preciousness. This can happen verbally, mentally, emotionally, spiritually, or sexually. In our pain story, we unlock and discover what those violations are, and who committed them against us. When someone crosses a boundary, misuses power, or fails to honor our basic humanity, we receive messages such as:

"You're not safe."

"You don't matter."

"You're too much—or not enough."

These are once again shame messages. They don't always come through harsh words or open conflict. In fact, they're often unspoken, felt through silence or the absence of care. They take shape in a glance of disapproval, in chronic neglect, in betrayal or manipulation. And over time, they settle into our nervous system. They become embedded in our sense of identity.

Violations are not always loud. More often, they're subtle, quiet, and persistent. And unless we name them, we continue to live under their influence. This shows up in a variety of ways, including:

- Verbal: harsh criticism, sarcasm, mocking, passive-aggressive words
- Emotional: gas-lighting, emotional neglect, manipulation, invalidation
- Spiritual: using Scripture or faith to shame, silence, or control
- Sexual: unwanted touch, exposure, coercion—even in "safe" relationships
- Relational: betrayal, inconsistency, emotional absence from trusted people
- Systemic: growing up in environments marked by injustice, poverty, or silence around pain

Copyright Spirit of Life Recovery. All Rights Reserved.

WHEN WHAT'S MISSING BECOMES THE WOUND

Not all violations stem from overt actions or what others did to us. Sometimes, the most profound pain comes from what didn't happen—the absence of care, attention, and validation that we needed but never received. Growing up in environments where emotional support was lacking, healthy modeling was absent, or spiritual safety was never established can leave invisible scars. Often, we may not have recognized this as trauma at the time, especially when there were no outward signs to point to. We may have been told that we were "fine" or expected to simply cope without being shown how to handle or express our emotions. But the absence of these vital elements of care is still a wound, a gaping hole in our hearts that shapes how we view ourselves and the world around us.

If we had to:

- Suppress our needs to keep the peace: We learned to push down our own feelings to avoid conflict, to make others comfortable, to maintain harmony at all costs. Our needs were silenced, and in doing so, we lost the ability to recognize and honor our own worth.

- Become the caretaker before we had a childhood: Instead of being nurtured, we took on roles that were too big for us. We cared for others, often at the expense of our own emotional and developmental needs, feeling responsible for their happiness, safety, or well-being.

- Stay strong so others wouldn't fall apart: We adopted the belief that we couldn't be vulnerable, that showing our own weakness would cause others to crumble. We became the rock, the one who never cracked, and in doing so, we buried our own hurt and grief.

- Hide our emotions to be accepted: We learned to mask our true feelings to fit in, to avoid being judged or rejected. Our authenticity was replaced by a carefully constructed persona, and we became accustomed to hiding the pain that no one seemed to notice.

In each of these scenarios, we were shaped by emotional absence—by the things that were missing, the needs that were left unmet. And absence, just like active harm, can wound us just as deeply. It's not a wound that's easy to identify because it's not the result of something that was done to us directly; it's the result of what was never given to us. The absence of nurturing, safety, and emotional expression creates a void in our soul that can be just as harmful as any overt abuse.

Acknowledging our unmet needs doesn't make us weak or needy—it makes us wise. It's a powerful step in the healing journey. When we begin to recognize the places where we were neglected, where our needs were dismissed or unseen, we open ourselves up to the possibility of restoration. We create space for God to enter into those wounds, to rewrite the story with His truth and love. In this sacred process, God doesn't just patch up the old, broken parts; He heals them, filling in the gaps with His presence, His care, and His unconditional love.

Healing begins when we dare to face the absence and acknowledge it. Only then can we start to see the truth of who we really are—worthy, loved, and deserving of care and attention. And in doing so, we create room for God to show us the abundant love and grace we were always meant to receive.

Copyright Spirit of Life Recovery. All Rights Reserved.

GRACE TO FORGIVE

Since we can't change the past, how can we rewire our hearts to view the same set of circumstances in a healing and redemptive way? Simply put, we need to retrieve God's perspective and rely on His resources. One of the most powerful resources He offers us is forgiveness—both receiving it for our own failures and extending it to those who have harmed us. But forgiveness doesn't happen instantly. It's more important to first feel and understand the nature of the damage done than to simply place forgiveness on the wound. Saying "I forgive _____" without processing the pain can often be a band-aid rather than a true remedy.

THE PROCESS OF FORGIVENESS

Once we comprehend the violation, the next vital step is recognizing that forgiveness is not the same as allowance. It isn't about justifying or minimizing what someone has done. In fact, until we grasp the depth of pain inflicted and the shame that has been perpetuated, we aren't truly ready to forgive. Forgiveness happens when we face the full weight of a violation. That's why it's often avoided—we tend to cover the wound with anger, disconnection, codependence, addiction, or other distractions. But real healing comes when we face the pain head-on.

Forgiveness begins by separating the person from their behavior. Jesus loved us but despised the shame He endured on the cross. He didn't condone our sin, but He bore its consequences so we could be free. In the same way, forgiveness calls us to release the person, while still hating the behavior that caused the harm. To undo shame, we must affirm the value of human life—even when we aren't aligned or in agreement with those who brought us pain. At the same time, we must resist the urge to process violations through shame, which often leads us to impute judgment, hostility, and punishment. When we place ourselves in the role of judge and juror, determining how someone should pay for what they've done, we remain trapped under the force of shame. It continues to define us and drive us, often leaking into other areas of our lives.

DISCHARGING SHAME

The Greek word for "forgive," *aphēte*, means "to release" or "to send away." When we forgive, we surrender our right to retaliate and no longer carry the weight of shame or a self-appointed duty to punish. We discharge that person to Jesus instead of taking matters into our own hands.

So, what does it mean for God to be the judge? It doesn't mean that grace automatically wipes the slate clean. Grace is activated when a person humbly admits their wrongdoing to God and asks Him to absorb the shame by His mercy. It is God's role to deal with that person—He is the righteous judge. Scripture says He will not be mocked, and that people will reap what they sow. When someone commits an injustice against us, we return that person to God and trust Him to manage the outcome. That person remains accountable to God for what they did or failed to do in relationship with us. Grace becomes theirs when they come to Him in repentance. Until then, they are still fully accountable to Him—there is no free pass.

Many of us mistake forgiveness for indifference, as though letting go means what they did didn't matter. But forgiveness isn't about minimizing pain. It simply means we choose not to carry the judgment and weight of that act any longer. It has already done enough damage. We don't want it to define or hurt us anymore, so we release it. And God, in His love and righteousness, accepts what we surrender to Him. Never underestimate what happens when we entrust people to God.

FORGIVENESS AND RECONCILIATION

Just because we forgive doesn't mean we are stepping into reconciliation. Forgiveness does not guarantee restoration of relationship or the return to the same relational dynamics. It simply means we are no longer operating in resentment, shame, or punishment. Forgiveness strips the power and authority that sin or trauma had over us. Reconciliation is another matter entirely. If someone refuses to take responsibility for their actions, reconciliation may not be possible. However, if reconciliation is desired, it becomes a possibility only when that person is willing to own their part and seek healing.

Relationships often shift after genuine healing. This may look like:

- Forgiving but leaving the relationship permanently

- Forgiving while setting new and clear boundaries

- Forgiving and, with repentance, rebuilding a relationship based on grace

Healthy boundaries can be established after forgiveness. Before forgiveness, boundaries often fail to work because they're driven by unresolved resentment, fear, intimidation, or weakness. To truly apply forgiveness to your situation, take time to reflect on the nature of the event before rushing to forgive. A worksheet is included at the end of this resource to help guide you through the forgiveness principles covered here.

HEALING PERPETRATOR ROOTS

Pain lies at the core of the victim experience. And when that pain goes unhealed, it often morphs into something far more destructive. Left unchecked, pain invites in resentment, bitterness, and even hate. In time, the victim may become what they once despised—a perpetrator.

This may seem unthinkable at first, but it's not uncommon. We cannot underestimate the power of shame and unforgiveness. The longer these forces are left to operate in silence, the more they warp the human heart.

Learning to see ourselves or others as perpetrators is hard. We must never use this label to form core identities—it is a style of survival or a behavior. It's also what happens when the human heart is regulated by shame and sin, instead of grace and redemption. This is why we want to expose shame and see where control comes into play.

We want to release resentment, so we resist the urge to bring people into our own forms of judgment. We want to see people the way God sees people. If we don't let God heal, we are prone to recycle shame and end up placing that shame onto others. But when we open our hearts and become tender to the reality of forgiveness and acceptance, we can be set free.

JONAS'S STORY: THE HIDDEN PERPETRATOR

Jonas carried deep wounds from his father. Growing up under verbal and emotional abuse, he lived much of his early life as a victim. As an adult, he revisited those painful memories and began the journey of healing. But in the present, the relationship with his father was still strained.

Now elderly and suffering from dementia, his father no longer had the power to inflict harm. But Jonas had resentment—years of it. And that resentment turned to hate. He began calling his father names, using every opportunity to remind him of his failures. He made sure his father felt the sting of guilt and regret.

In his mind, Jonas was finally powerful. But in his heart, he had become a perpetrator—using shame as a weapon. What Jonas didn't realize at first was that his father had also been a victim of abuse. Though it didn't excuse his actions, it gave context.

Jonas believed his actions were justified. He wanted his father to feel the weight of what he had done. But in seeking repayment, Jonas had crossed the line. He grieved God's heart—not because he felt pain, but because he refused to let grace in.

When God began to heal Jonas's heart, everything changed. He saw his father not as an enemy, but as a broken man. Jonas asked for forgiveness—not just from God, but from his father. Though his father could barely comprehend it, the act itself became healing for Jonas.

Jonas became an advocate for his father's care. He tended to his needs. He made peace, not because his father had earned it, but because grace had changed him.

And in doing so, Jonas removed shame's power—not just from himself, but from the story as a whole. He left behind vengeance and carried the light of Jesus into a dark legacy. That is what grace can do.

THE PERPETRATOR'S NEED FOR GRACE

However perpetration plays out, when we are the carrier of wrongdoing, we can either be gripped with shame and guilt, or be totally disconnected and hardened. Some of the most morally right people in the world are the most hateful in their heart. They focus on external goodness, but they lack any grace.

What's most important for right now is that we take ownership of our part. It doesn't negate the wrongdoers or minimize the reality for boundaries. It simply enables our own heart to remain pure.

However, we must be careful that we don't overly focus on our mistakes and wrongdoing. If we become overwhelmed by guilt and shame, we aren't benefiting from grace. Grace removes our sin and shame as we confess our wrongdoing. The very reason the cross exists is because we can't undo our wrongs. Thus, God grants us a cleansing from all past wrongdoings.

Consequences aren't removed by grace, but the heavy load of guilt and shame can be totally taken away. In fact, someone can sit in an actual prison cell because of a crime they committed, but through grace, that prison cell can be a place of freedom, rest, love, and value.

That's how powerful grace is—it sets the soul free and allows union and fellowship with King Jesus. Perpetrators desperately need grace. If they are in denial, they also need boundaries (we will look at this later). There is no amount of self-guilt or self-condemnation that is acceptable. Grace covers perpetration. Actions to repair the wrongs are a separate transaction.

God's requirement to access grace is minimal. He asks that we confess, which is another way of saying we come into agreement with God's point of view. Then we repent and receive forgiveness. Repenting is a change—and at this point, the only change that matters is that we believe in grace as the remedy. Receiving is the power of grace to change us from here on out. This is gradual transformation that takes time and happens day in and day out.

In the immediate situation of finding our shame thoughts, we can learn to develop a power statement to tame shame's influence and remind shame that grace is the boss. This takes a constant commitment and awareness. If we automatically respond to shame, we will let shame continue to decimate our progress. If we include grace, we can begin the transformation process.

Power Statements:

Even though I _____ to _____, I am still loved, valued and accepted by God.

Even though I _____, I can still be forgiven.

The power statement doesn't take away the wrongdoing. But it repairs the inner foundation of the heart and allows for a new lifestyle to be formed. It about the burden released, the debt paid and the receiving of grace in the place of shame's horrific reality.

WHEN PERPETRATORS CHOOSE PRIDE

The flip side of shame is pride. Pride elevates a person above another through a false sense of their own goodness or power. It gives the illusion of security by building a false sense of worth based on perceived traits that outshine others or feed self-righteous standards. Prideful people often resist being wrong and operate in constant defensiveness to protect their self-image. Whether it takes on a religious tone with Christian overtones or reveals itself in more overtly immoral behaviors, pride always acts as a block to grace.

When someone operates from pride, connection—with Jesus or others—is cut off. That's why the only way to engage with a prideful person, especially when they are unaware of their predatory tendencies, is through boundaries. We'll explore how to do this in a later section, but for now, it's important to understand that we are not powerless just because someone is prideful. Pride is the fruit of a deeper issue, and it thrives on convincing us that it is right and we are wrong. We must refuse to live under that illusion, even while recognizing that we do not have the ability to open blind eyes.

If we're not careful, we may try to deal with someone's pride and controlling behavior by attempting to control them in return. But once we do that—once we try to manage another person's heart directly—we interrupt the flow of grace in our own healing process. We also block grace from reaching into that relationship. Grace is not just about transforming someone else. It's about allowing God to change us so we can see clearly and respond rightly. Sometimes grace will lead us to set boundaries. Sometimes it will ask us to walk away. Other times, God's plan involves restoration. The most difficult part is surrendering the outcome to Him.

We are called to forgive the perpetrator, but that doesn't mean we allow them continued access to harm us. We'll explore that more in the next section. But as we begin the process, we must ground ourselves in truth:

Power Statement
Even though _____ does _____, I am still loved, valued, and accepted by God. Therefore, I do not live under their pride. I release _____ to You, Lord. I give up the right to control or fix them.

RESCUERS IN THE HEALING JOURNEY

While the roles of victim and perpetrator are often clear-cut, the rescuer's role is more abstract. If we were rescuers, we likely became accustomed to bearing the burdens of others. If we sought rescuers, we may have developed a pattern of placing people on pedestals—only to feel betrayed or disappointed when they eventually failed us. In both scenarios, what we truly need is to stabilize the part of us that desires to rescue or be rescued. This desire reflects a lack of power and resources, revealing our deep need to control outcomes and change the people around us. While victims and perpetrators need forgiveness, the rescuer needs surrender.

What's surprising is that rescuing, though seemingly well-intentioned, overlaps with predatory behavior. Anytime we try to change someone, we step into a form of perpetration. That realization can be shocking. When we attempt to control or "fix" another person, we interfere with God's ability to intervene in their life. For the rescuer, hearing the words "I don't need you" can feel terrifying. But when those words come from Jesus, they carry a liberating truth. He says, "I don't need you anymore"—not as rejection, but as an invitation to step aside and let Him take His rightful place. Being a rescuer often blocks Jesus from doing what only He can do. Yet, in His tenderness, He understands how hard it is to surrender this role. It takes time and intimacy with Jesus to fully trust His heart and release control to Him.

When we've relied on someone else to rescue us, we've placed strain on the relationship by assigning them a role only God can fulfill—and likely punished them when they failed. We need to repent of this cycle and examine the unrealistic expectations we've placed on others. Unintentionally, we've stepped into the role of perpetrator ourselves. And when we've taken on the role of rescuer, our desire to save others—while noble in appearance—is ultimately an attempt to stand in God's place. That, too, requires repentance. Even though it may not seem like a violation, if it prevents someone from experiencing the power of Jesus, it becomes one.

Rescuing can look innocent—even noble—but it's one of the positions that most competes with Jesus. Therefore, we must become willing to recognize it for what it is. Releasing the rescuer is about relinquishing personal power and allowing Jesus to lead. While repentance is an essential part of that journey, there's an even deeper need for love and security. God understands the motivations behind the rescuer's heart—our longing to bring stability, prevent failure, and help others. These desires are rooted in goodness, which is why rescuers need more than just correction. They need better tools and a sense of empowerment that comes from God. Later, we'll explore how to replace rescuing tendencies with grace-based boundaries and strength.

Even though I rescued _____, I am loved, valued, and accepted by God. I can let _____ be rescued by Jesus.

OR

Even though I tried to be rescued by _____, I am loved, valued, and accepted by God. I can be rescued by Jesus.

These power statements may seem small and simple, but they have the potential to transform from the inside out.

GIVING OURSELVES GRACE

As we examine the cycles of pain, we often realize that what we lacked most was grace. Yet receiving grace takes time. One of the most important realizations we can have in the present moment is our own limitations. We are human—and that means we cannot meet the standards that this world or our relationships have imposed on us. Even on our best day, we fall short in many ways. Shame causes us to impose standards on ourselves like a slave master. When we impose unrealistic expectations on our lives, we set ourselves up for failure and shame. And out of that shame, we fall into the same relational traps and emotional reactions we're trying to escape.

The way to break this cycle is by receiving grace—allowing Jesus to manage our brokenness—and then extending that grace to ourselves. If Jesus accepts us in our weaknesses, we must begin to apply that same grace to the parts of ourselves we often reject. The pressure to live up to a personal standard of how we should look, behave, or perform in relationships is what has hurt us the most. But when we realize that Jesus accepts us as we are, we gain permission to accept ourselves too.

There is nothing spiritual about self-punishment. Keeping ourselves on the hook and sabotaging our capacity to receive grace doesn't just harm us—it harms those around us, who miss out on the beauty of grace living and flowing through us. The power statement that follows may be the most important one you can carry into your life. It applies to any place where you feel you are falling short, failing, or living beneath your potential.

Even though I don't feel I'm measuring up in _____, I am loved and accepted by God. Therefore, I can love and accept myself.

WHEN MORE HELP IS NEEDED

For some, the content in this chapter will spark new awareness and bring freedom. For others, especially those with a history of trauma, this process may feel overwhelming. That's okay.

Find a trauma-informed counselor or a ministry that offers Christ-centered healing (visit www.spiritofliferecovery.com). Look for a counselor who understands both the emotional and spiritual components of your story. You are worth the investment. Your inner world deserves to be free.

Worksheet: Forgiveness (Page 47)

Boundaries & Breaking Cycles of Pain

FORGIVENESS WORKSHEET

Describe the details of the violation or the reality of unmet needs:
_____
_____
_____
_____

This is how it made me feel:
_____
_____
_____
_____

This is how I responded a result:
_____
_____
_____
_____
_____
_____
_____

I separate _____ (name the person) from _____ (what they did to harm you).
I send _____ (name the person) back to you Jesus.

POWER STATEMENT
Even though _____ (name the person) hurt me, I am still loved, valued and accepted by God. Therefore, I can move on with my life.

How do I handle this relationship in the future?
_____ Forgive, but end the relationship or leave it in the past
_____ Forgive but set new power boundaries in the relationship (Part 4)
_____ Forgive and repair together (reconciliation)

PRAYER:
Father God,
I am hurt and feel overpowered by _____ because of _____. I know that you are more powerful, but in myself I am weak. I admit to you that I do not know how to let _____ off the hook. Truthfully, I don't feel they deserve it. But I trust that you are capable of giving me justice in this situation. I don't know what that looks lie, but you haven't given me the ability to make that happen. You've just asked me to trust you. Therefore, based on your character and your Word, I give _____ back to you. Help me with my control and need for vengeance. In Jesus name Amen

Copyright Spirit of Life Recovery. All Rights Reserved.

PART 4
Power Boundaries

The grace we receive comes in the form of acceptance, first from God and then with ourselves. Jesus adapted to our broken humanity by meeting us where we are, and we have to adapt to our humanity by accepting our own limits. We are imperfect. We have weaknesses, but God is perfectly satisfied with us. He will change us in time.

When we learn this, we can learn to offer this same perspective to others. Placing grace onto relationships doesn't mean we allow people to hurt or abuse us, however. We need to learn to walk with grace yet develop firm and powerful boundaries in relationships.

PRESENTING GRACE TO SHAME

Every strained relationship has two sides. One side is ours—how we respond, how we show up, and how we engage with the cycles of pain. The other side belongs to the person we're in relationship with—their pain, their coping strategies, and how they manage shame. When we understand that the roles people take on are formed systemically—often from wounds and unresolved hurt—we begin to gain insight. It doesn't excuse the damage they may have done, but it helps us see them with compassion. People are not just the sum of their behaviors. They carry stories. And much of what they do has less to do with us and more to do with their own internal war.

That doesn't make things easier. The human heart can still cause deep harm. But at the core of it all, every person is trying, consciously or unconsciously, to dissolve the power of shame. We were all created to live in love and freedom, but shame corrupts that purpose. There's a fine line between empathizing with someone's pain and using sympathy as an excuse to allow ongoing harm. Likewise, it's easy to respond to shame-based behavior with anger, control, or retaliation. Shame invites shame in return, and that cycle is hard to break. But Scripture offers us another way. It gives us profound insight into how to overcome the cycles of pain generated by shame. And it begins with a surprising solution.

Do not be overcome by evil, but overcome evil with good.— Romans 12:21

The word "evil" in this passage refers to inner malice or corruption. This is the very ingredient that fuels the shame cycle. It's not saying people are evil to the core—but rather, that the pain, dysfunction, and harmful behavior they carry can become tools of inner corruption. Left unchecked, shame turns into cycles of harm. Part of our challenge is that we're uncomfortable labeling normal human conflict as "malice" or "evil." But the truth is, when shame drives behavior, it creates destruction. And that internal struggle—whether in us or in someone else—is very real.

Copyright Spirit of Life Recovery. All Rights Reserved.

The second part of the verse tells us how to respond: conquer evil by doing good. That's more than just being nice. The original word for "good" here is the Greek word *agathos*. It means something empowered by God—goodness that originates in Him and flows through us. It's not a self-help solution; it's a grace-powered act of faith. In practical terms, this means we don't just muscle our way through relational hardship with willpower. We don't fake it until we make it. Instead, we allow God's grace to purify our own hearts first.

When we're in relationships where shame-based behavior or inner malice is present, it's tempting to call it out directly. But that can ignite more shame, defensiveness, or even retaliation. Grace doesn't pour gasoline on the fire. Grace pours water. That doesn't mean grace allows sin to continue unchecked. It means grace approaches differently, with strength and wisdom rooted in love.

Philippians 4:13 reminds us, "I can do all things through Christ who gives me strength". That strength is not from within ourselves. It's from God. It's His power that enables us to respond differently—to resist cycles of pain, to create healthy boundaries, and to move forward in peace.

Change doesn't come from striving. It comes from surrender. When God works in our hearts, we begin to choose differently. And in choosing differently, we become participants in breaking generational cycles of dysfunction, control, and shame.

WHAT GRACE ACCOMPLISHES

Before we inject grace into shame cycles, it's vital to understand the work it seeks to perform. Grace isn't conceptual; it is tangible power. It births transformation from the deepest place within us. It opens us to a new perspective where we can see ourselves and others through a new filter. Before we ever arrive or walk in grace, it's helpful to understand its ultimate agenda. While there is no limit to what grace can do, here are some of the attributes.

- **Grace teaches us our worth.** We begin to see ourselves the way God sees us—precious, loved, and valued. That identity gives us strength to walk away from abuse, to say no to mistreatment, and to stop tolerating what is harmful. When we know we are valuable, we can offer that same sense of worth to others—without enabling their dysfunction.

- **Grace restores our power to choose.** In shame, we feel stuck and powerless. In grace, we remember we have choices. Victims can step into freedom. Rescuers can let go of responsibility that was never theirs. Perpetrators can repent and take responsibility. No matter how hard, we always have a choice. Grace brings that choice back into focus.

- **Grace makes space for limitations.** We're not perfect. Other people aren't either. Grace allows us to accept that without living in denial or bitterness. Accepting someone's limitations doesn't mean we ignore unhealthy behavior—it just means we stop trying to change people who aren't ready to be changed. We accept reality and let God take the lead.

- **Grace provides the power to change.** God never convicts us without also equipping us. He doesn't just point out what's broken—He offers to heal and transform it. In the same way, we learn to leave the burden of changing others to Him. Grace reminds us that people don't change because we convince them. They change when God moves.

- **Grace helps us recognize and release unmet needs.** We all have needs, and not all of them get met by the people in our lives. Grace helps us grieve that honestly and then find our fulfillment in Jesus. It releases others from the pressure of being our savior, and it breaks the cycle of manipulation or emotional pressure.

- **Grace gives us security in Christ.** Even when the people in our lives are unstable, Jesus is our anchor. Sometimes God doesn't calm the storm around us—He calms the storm within us. He strengthens us in the middle of the mess. Grace gives us the ability to stay grounded, even when our relationships feel shaky.

- **Grace empowers us to set limits.** Just like Jesus sets boundaries in His relationship with us, we are allowed—and encouraged—to do the same. Limits are healthy. They are not punishments, but protections. Grace teaches us how to say no with love, how to set standards with wisdom, and how to hold the line without revenge.

The truth is, we don't mature in grace overnight. This is a journey. Grace becomes more natural as we abide in God's presence and walk in step with His Spirit. We don't perform grace—we receive it. And once it lives in us, it begins to overflow.

DEVELOPING BOUNDARY STRUCTURES FROM GRACE

So, how do we go from where we are—stuck in the cycles of pain—to using grace to build a new way forward? Usually, when we think of boundaries, we imagine how we handle other people's behavior. However, in a true sense, boundaries are about managing our own heart space to determine what we let in or keep out. Boundaries are built on our own property; in an internal sense, a boundary lives within our own heart. They guide and direct how we treat others and train other people on how to treat us.

The cycles of pain carry profoundly toxic boundary structures. Everyone is simply surviving with no solid sense of right or wrong—no understanding of individual rights or justice. People reach into our world and disrespect and violate us in various ways. Sometimes, we do the same thing in return. Powerlessness and shame drive this cycle as everyone moves through different roles: victim, perpetrator, and rescuer. No one can understand their role; instead, they focus on others. This lack of personal ownership, responsibility, and validation of truth makes breaking these cycles impossible.

The first—and only—way to change is to recognize that the cycle itself is wrong. This requires breaking denial and receiving truth; it is the hardest obstacle we will face. It is easier to maintain the position of victim, perpetrator, or rescuer—it's easier to blame others. That system has already developed naturally within us.

Copyright Spirit of Life Recovery. All Rights Reserved.

Think of a field with a beaten-down track running through the middle; it feels natural to want to follow that established pathway. If you had to prepare a new path, it would take repetition and intention to do so. Your brain and mind become accustomed to responding in certain ways, and thus they have been trained for automatic responses based on learned behaviors and the brain's memory.

Staking out a new pathway can be hard work. What makes it even more difficult is that new responses may not directly change the other person at all initially—but the goal is to break free from the cycle of pain within yourself while finding healthier means of relating going forward.

It will be natural—and normal—to fail at responding differently at first because true change takes time! However, the key lies in beginning by owning your story honestly before both yourself and God regarding how you have managed relationships thus far so that you can then position yourself for implementing new strategies effectively moving forward.

To apply boundaries to cycles of pain, we must set these core elements in place:

- Boundaries are based on the truth that everyone is lovable, valuable, and acceptable, even if behaviors aren't.
- Everyone has the right to be loved, valued, and accepted in relationships. That doesn't mean harmful behavior should be tolerated. Violations are actions or words that harm or disregard our well-being.

There are many types of violations, and we will explore how to manage them in more detail later.

Boundaries impose reasonable expectations.

Expectations can be driven by shame. We often place self-prescribed standards on others based on how we want them to act, think, or feel. We can reasonably expect kindness or safety, but we can't expect someone to be who they are not. High or unrealistic expectations often violate others by demanding more than they can give. Grace means accepting where people are, even if we wish they were somewhere else.

Boundaries validate the needs and feelings of everyone.

Relationships require both people to give and receive. Everyone is entitled to needs, but those needs must be communicated fairly. Control, guilt, or shaming to get our needs met is not grace-based. Needs must be processed in our heart and expressed with clarity.

Feelings are also valid, but not all feelings are truthful or should be expressed harmfully. Healthy communication uses "I" statements like: "I feel hurt when you ignore me." We must avoid saying, "You made me feel…" because that implies someone else controls our emotional state. Expressing feelings is about creating connection, not forcing outcomes. Vulnerability gives our feelings a voice; withholding them keeps us isolated.

Boundaries give us the ability to say "I can."

When someone repeatedly hurts or violates us, we have the right to respond with action. We can set consequences that stop the behavior. But we must be willing to live with those consequences. If fear keeps us from enforcing boundaries, we stay powerless.

Choosing to act, rather than react, gives us a sense of control rooted in grace. "I can" statements are powerful tools that move us toward freedom.

Using these core ingredients, we will learn to apply grace-based boundaries to the victim, perpetrator, and rescuer roles within cycles of pain. Through these action steps, we can find real-life application and begin rewriting our story from a place of truth and empowerment.

BREAKING VICTIM CYCLES

The victim role stands for powerlessness, so leaving the victim role is about being empowered through the rightful resource of grace. Living empowered by Jesus is an internal state of being. Faulty healing happens when the victim role merges into a position of anger and revenge. While anger is a normal part of healing, it isn't the ending point. Instead, the victim heals by receiving the inner perspective of Jesus. The validation of the plight of the victim is one of the greatest needs.

If, as a victim, we become overly aggressive to make up for the state of feeling oppressed, we switch to another role inside the same cycle. This doesn't birth freedom. The goal of real healing is to walk in paths of peace, truth, righteousness, and forgiveness. It is the freedom to make better choices and not repeat cycles. It is a state of having shame rid permanently and being altered in the deepest place of worth and identity.

From internal healing, we can gain our rights and privileges as a child of God. This doesn't mean we can use anger, shame, blame, or other toxic tools to combat the violations. Instead, we need to face our own perspective and honestly assess what is happening within.

When we feel a sense of violation or offense, we don't dodge it, deny it, or fight. Instead, we can confront it. Healthy confrontation is something most of us in cycles of pain never learned. We learned to work around the problem instead of facing it head-on. We learned that speaking real feelings wasn't perhaps acceptable or safe. But through the strategies of grace, we need to actually confront the issue as it is, without putting any filters on it—and without the use of control. Healthy confrontation allows us to express what we don't like or won't allow, and also states how it affects us.

APPLYING BOUNDARIES

Jack and Jody were constantly at war with each other. Jody always felt overpowered by Jack's chronic abusive language. He insisted on being right and being above her in opinions. This left Jody feeling devalued, unimportant, and misunderstood. When Jody fought for a voice, Jack fought harder.

Copyright Spirit of Life Recovery. All Rights Reserved.

Jody's own healing process had to help her see the cycle. She had to recognize her own woundedness inside herself, both past and present. She also needed to understand that Jack carried his own issues that had nothing to do with her. Instead of demonizing him as the enemy, she could begin to understand he manifested his participation in cycles of shame due to his personal experience.

Should Jody never process her perspective of her husband with Jesus, she might expect her husband to change before she can make relational adjustments. When Jody recognizes that she is in the role of a powerless victim, she has the capacity to learn a new power structure to drive her life.

ADDING GRACE

We will look at ways to insert grace into the victim cycle. These same steps are valid for each role we cover, but they contain unique features depending on what role we are facing. Grabbing onto grace isn't a religious process; it's a matter of housing it authentically in order to offer it. And this can be an internal war. That's why we need prayer and intimacy with King Jesus to even gain the tools to apply these principles. When we don't know where to go or how to gain access, we can always seek Jesus. From there, we can apply some practical solutions.

Using Jody's situation, we are going to look at how we actually can apply grace with tangible steps.

LOVE, VALUE & ACCEPTANCE

Jody needs to gain the power of grace before she has it in her to heal. Since she is combating shame and inner unworthiness more than anything else, she can start with a power statement. The power statement is where Jody generates her internal worth. It is the statement she makes about who she is despite what Jack does or says.

Example: "Even though Jack is controlling, I am loved, valued, and accepted by God."

Although a power statement isn't an instant cure, it is a reminder of the work of healing God is doing in her and can stabilize her perspective. Jody might sit inside this space for some time before finding the strength to enter into confrontation.

EXPECTATIONS

Jody needs to understand that her husband is prone to error. He is far from perfect, and can't turn into Prince Charming overnight. Instead, he needs room to be broken in his own ways. She can pray for him on the basis of his worth and love, not just on what he's doing wrong.

NEEDS & FEELINGS

The cycles of pain are based on unspoken needs and power attempts to get those needs met. To counter that, truth and honest feelings need to be spoken. Jody needs to acknowledge her feelings internally by spending time with Jesus. Being honest inside her own heart is the biggest battle. But then she needs to express those same feelings to Jack.

Jack may not validate them and may even be critical or demeaning. But that isn't the point. Her ability to express the truth of her pain is confronting the problem as it is with honesty and words that allow Jack to see her humanity.

Example: "Jack, when you talk to me in a rude way, I feel sad and unimportant." Jody can share in direct terms what her needs are: "I need kind communication and to feel understood."

I CAN RESPONSE

Jody now understands that she has choices. These are options she has to overcome evil with good. Should she retaliate, shame, blame, judge, or punish, she retains her own bondage. But if she can choose to find healthy strategies, she cuts Jack off from being powerful over her.

Jody's "I can" statements may include:

- I can choose to leave the conversation
- I can choose to leave the room
- I can choose to guard my heart
- I can choose to set parameters with language that I consider abusive
- I can choose to find help to process the pain
- I can join a support group
- I can choose to no longer tolerate the cycle in this relationship and leave it without further changes being offered

The solutions Jody places on the situation don't change Jack. They don't scold him or punish him either. Rather, they end the cycle.

Powerlessness is always a lie. It is never about lacking choices; it's about being willing to make choices that go against the grain of that relational cycle. But learning to walk in God's power requires honest humility. God operates by love—even when it's confrontational.

Jesus modeled to us the power to forgive in the face of evil. This is the actual power to break cycles and strongholds. Jesus came to give us power. The end result of all confrontation is never to punish or blame. It's always about the opportunity for forgiveness and restoration.

While restoration is the goal, without repentance, the relationship is stifled and experiences division. When someone is unwilling to own their part, boundaries remain in place. This is where decisions need to be made, decisions that only we and Jesus can ultimately decide.

APPLY

Use this model in your own relational struggle. Identify the current cycle you are in and how you feel victimized. Then work through the following:

Copyright Spirit of Life Recovery. All Rights Reserved.

- Who am I struggling with in relationship, and what is the source of strain? Why do I feel powerless?
- Have I processed through my heart issues that could be projected onto this situation? How can I gain access to more healing?
- What is my power statement to secure my worth and identity in Jesus?
- Have I been able to express the problem with the person involved? How might I incorporate a healthy approach to communication?

BREAKING RESCUER CYCLES

Rescuers fight shame with the tools of ennoblement and false power. Rescuers have no boundary established based on their inner world, but live life based on the perceived or real needs of others. They are influenced by learning to use their own "rescuing" power to fix the shame of others. But since the focus of help and aid comes in the form of focusing on others, they never find the power to apply to their own circumstances. The rescuer's greatest need is grace. And it is hard to access. Not because they are weak, but because the rescuer is, in fact, strong in their own strength.

It isn't that rescuers are malicious. They aren't. They are kind and usually seek justice. But they are going about it for the wrong reasons with the wrong tools. Rescuers invade other people's space by declaring they are stronger than another person's problems, and thus have the resources to fix it. This prevents the person from gaining the tools and skills to manage their problems directly with God.

A rescuer's breakthrough is, therefore, the ability to understand the wrongful role they play and the willingness to surrender. But since the rescuer has developed an entire system to learn life, finding personal boundaries and forging new pathways and a new way of managing problems is highly difficult. In our own cycles with rescuing, we need to identify that we have the issue in the first place.

Then, we need to learn that our intentions are correct, but our strategies are faulty. Trying to play the role of savior to people in difficult spaces is oftentimes competing with God. God is the source for people; we are only vessels that carry a resource that will lead people back to Him.

There is a fine line between help that allows people to find solutions and help that prevents them from finding the answers through their own choices. Choices are what help us forge new pathways in our minds and hearts. But those pathways are under our individual jurisdiction. We don't have permission to try to create internal pathways inside other people's minds or hearts. To do so would be an utter violation of free will.

Thus, our greatest task is to develop partnership with King Jesus to simply participate as He allows, and to let go when necessary. We are only there to be used by Him, not to replace the work He needs to do directly.

APPLYING BOUNDARIES

John was excessively involved with his son Eric's problems with addiction and crime. In many ways, John held onto the shame that he had not been an effective parent, and thus he took responsibility

Copyright Spirit of Life Recovery. All Rights Reserved.

for Eric's problems. This responsibility gave him a false sense of ownership for his son's choices. This caused him to rescue his son, to bail him out of jail, to give him money, and to constantly "coddle" his bad choices.

While John thought these acts of love helped his son, they only allowed his son to retain his perpetrator role. In truth, John's son was making terrible choices and needed accountability. Instead, John bore the shame on behalf of his son in an act of martyrdom that dismantled God's ability to help Eric. John never meant harm. His intentions were entirely good. But they were deceptive and brought far more harm than good.

For John, his main hurdle was seeing that this role was faulty. He then would have to understand what was happening inside his own heart, and what he himself needed to heal so that shame's power could be dismantled. This always proves the hardest spot for a rescuer, because they are obsessed with using themselves as a vehicle for the needs of others, rather than having to look and face their pain within.

Then, John would need wisdom to understand how to separate his role from God's role, and how to help his son in a way that benefits the outcome, rather than remain stuck by fear and shame. John needs supernatural grace. He doesn't own this in his own strength. It is a resource God must provide to him, and John is faced with the dramatic task of surrender.

These cycles can be so hard to break that a support group may be required to help walk those early steps. People have to break rescuing roles at the same level that addictions are broken. It holds incredible power, more than we can imagine as we try to walk away. It's okay to need additional support. It's part of the resources God provides to us on our journey toward healing.

ADDING GRACE

#1. LOVE, VALUE & ACCEPTANCE

John needs the power of grace to rewrite the internal shame and guilt he harbored. He needs to face that this was the root issue driving him to rescue in the first place. Every parent fails, and John needs to accept that his failure had to be released and the power of it dismantled. He might even learn that he has overly blamed himself for just being a human being. Therefore, he needs to speak into that lie by declaring the power statement.

"Even if I have failed as a parent, I am still loved, valued, and accepted by God."

At first, this may mean little to John's heart. But he is working to establish a new "normal" in his inner world. If John can be let off the hook for his shame, it will no longer power the engine of the cycle of shame with Eric.

#2. EXPECTATIONS

John needs to learn to handle the expectations he placed on himself and the lack of expectations he placed on his son. He learned to over-perform while his son had been allowed to under-perform. In both cases, the expectations marred the need for grace and help. Through grace, John can allow God to help him in his weakness. And trust God to help Eric rise up to a level that would lead to growth. If Eric doesn't do that, John can still love him where he's at, realizing that it is God's job to take over.

#3. NEEDS & FEELINGS

John has to identify the real emotion behind the rescuing. He also has to understand what is happening with Eric. Eric is making bad choices, and John is protecting Eric from facing that. Therefore, John has to recognize his own emotions and also recognize the faulty role he had played. This will better help him communicate the issue with Eric. That root is based on shame and fear. He deals with the shame with God, but the fear is something he can express to his son.

"Son, when you are out using and participating in devastating behavior my heart literally breaks and I feel so sad."

This is an honest dialogue of what is actually happening in his heart. It explains why he rescues and his loving concern. He can share this instead of avoiding it and resorting to strategies of rescuing.

John must also be honest about the needs driving his rescuing behavior. Perhaps he needs to feel needed or fears being a bad parent. Maybe he needs validation or fears rejection if he lets go. These are legitimate emotional needs, but they must be brought into the light, surrendered to God, and not allowed to drive decisions. John needs to sit with questions like:

- What emotional need am I trying to fill by rescuing?
- Am I afraid of being rejected or unloved if I don't help?
- Do I feel guilty or ashamed for not doing enough?
- What do I need from God to fill this space?

He also needs to learn how to express his needs to Eric when appropriate. This does not mean Eric is responsible for meeting those needs, but it models healthy vulnerability. For example, "Eric, I need to know that you're willing to take responsibility for your life. I need to trust that you will do what's right, not just for me, but for yourself."

This is met with resistance when someone has been benefiting from the rescuer's help for a long period of time. It will be hard to detach from this initially, and the fight can be profound. John's job is to let Eric take back the responsibility of choices. He might have to admit to Eric that he has been wrongfully rescuing. Now it is Eric's job to make decisions on how to resolve the problem with God's help, not John's. John can aid with help if Eric is leading the way in decision-making. He doesn't have to just drop him. But his mission is to encourage his son to choose things for himself and retain the consequences, rather than John managing his life for him. By doing this, John is helping his son create a new pathway inside of himself instead of leaning on his dad's decisions. This will let Eric become stronger and hopefully find healing.

Just because Eric can make better decisions doesn't mean he will. There is a terrifying space of letting go where we have to let a person fail. If the person is in a life-threatening situation, we can, of course, intervene. But we need to take the power of grace we ourselves ingest and become warriors behind the scenes, trusting God rather than our efforts. Our new rescuing task is to pray and stand in the gap through intercession rather than managing circumstances. This letting go is at the heart of the struggle the rescuer will have to face. It is also where freedom will be birthed.

#4. I CAN RESPONSE

John can do other things to help his son when shame has been dismantled and he's not driven by the need to take over. These decisions will prove to be a vital part of John's long-term recovery. John will feel stress for what he can't do. He will feel scared and frustrated that he needs to stop being Eric's source of help. That's why it's vital for John to develop some plans based on "I can" statements.

- I can hold my son accountable for his own decisions and stop bailing him out so he can learn life's lessons directly.
- I can tell my son I am sorry for past hurts, but then let it go.
- I can help my son in positive ways that will lead to his well-being if God is leading me first.
- I can stop controlling and rescuing my son.
- I can trust God with my son and leave the outcomes up to Him.
- I can receive forgiveness for my wrongdoing.
- I can forgive myself.
- I can find a support group.
- I can pray for my son all the time.

The "I can" of Christianity is, many times, the death of our inward need to fix and control. It will be an internal battle. This breaking of cycles may require other resources because the switch to a healthier mindset involves John's personal journey of healing. He may need to sit in meetings that help him understand other parents' plight. However he does that, he can understand that putting down his role of rescuing is not the lack of love for Eric. It holds deep love for his son, but it is a love that entrusts the power of God more than his own efforts to birth change.

APPLY

Use this model in your own relational struggle. Identify the current cycle you are in and how you feel victimized. Then work through the following:

- Do I try to rescue people in relationships? Who? Why do I do this?
- What is my power statement to secure my worth and identity in Jesus?
- Have I been able to express the problem with the person involved?
- How might I incorporate a "When you do _____ I feel _____" statement?
- What are the blocks or reasons I can't?
- What "I can" statements can I make?
- Do I need to secure more support for myself? Where and how?

BREAKING PERPETRATOR CYCLES

Perpetrators carry the "ugly" behavior of more advanced forms of control. True perpetrators operate through false strategies of power and give little concern to the needs of others. The biggest challenge perpetrators face is that they naturally don't come under the sense that shame is bad—they partner with it, thus they don't feel under its domination and force. Because the people in their lives have adapted to aggressive forms of control, anger, threats, shame, and fear, the presence of these behaviors has been normalized. This allows perpetrators to retain this position without consequence. Everyone is stuck inside the cycle.

Perpetrators need someone to stand against the bullying mentality with boundaries to even see or comprehend what they are doing isn't acceptable. This is why it's the job of the victim to set those standards. Without them, no guidance is being offered, and no standards are set. Some perpetrators will continue to violate anyways, and those that are fully engulfed in selfish and abusive cycles need more severe consequences. That is up to the people that the perpetrator is offending to determine those consequences. If perpetrators are continually allowed to use those tactics and they are effective, they are rewarded and empowered.

In our own lives, we can be blinded to the role of the perpetrator that we ourselves carry. We can see ourselves as a victim, so we have no capacity to view ourselves as participating in cycles of pain wrongfully. But when we have shame reactions that come out in the form of anger, rage, words of judgment, accusation, blame, or punishment, we are acting from a perpetrator mentality. Perpetrators lack boundary structure because they operate by crushing a person's right and taking over their point of view. They feel entitled to tell a person who they are, what they should do, how they should feel, and how they should act. Anytime we house that mindset, we are standing in the role of a perpetrator.

Where victims have a powerless problem, perpetrators have a power problem. They use power to ride over people. Words are as much a weapon as actions in perpetrators, being used to break down, hurt, and injure those that come under their influence.

What perpetrators actually need is grace to be healed and mended from within. But to get there, they need to see their wrongdoing. Thus, the goal of their healing will be to enter into a state of repentance.

In our own hearts, the boundaries we need to rebuild come in the form of assessing our own hearts and seeing when we use tactics of power wrongfully. Even if we are defending ourselves from perpetrators, we are only fueling the wrongdoing. Overcoming evil with good is a state of not participating in cycles that contain "tearing down." We don't have to ignore what is happening, but we don't engage and break people to make our points known.

APPLYING BOUNDARIES

Jan had excessive abuse in her childhood and married an abusive husband. After years of anguish and profound distress, Jan was set free from that terrible cycle. Wounded and hurt, Jan was cynical of all men and people in general. Her inward pain was never managed through the power of grace, thus she housed shame and anger as a result. Jan's original wounds are tragic. They deserve validation and understanding. But as she grew older, she became hardened and resentful. Instead of making herself vulnerable to future pain, Jan took on the position of being controlling and bossy in all her dealings with people. In her job and position in church, Jan had little care or empathy in her approaches. She tolerated nothing from people and let them know in plain terms when they did things wrong. When she remarried, she found a weaker husband who would not talk back to her. She ran the relationship and demeaned and berated him on a regular basis. He received this role because he had learned the victim role as a means of survival.

When Jan's world spiraled out of control again, she became willing to own responsibility for her choices. To heal, she needed to revisit the past (See Part 3). It was vital that she faced original wounds and gave them the proper care and attention. In the here and now, she had to learn that she, in fact, was a perpetrator. Her wounds had caused her to switch roles within the cycle of pain. She hurt people and used sharp and painful words to assault people's dignity. This came from the root of shame she herself carried.

Jan would have to learn to see herself in two ways. The first is that she sees her own preciousness and value as God sees her. The next is that she is aware of her perpetrator part that wants to use retaliation and control to hurt others when she is hurt.

Perpetrators don't have the luxury of letting themselves off the hook easily. They have to be honest about their inner tendency to be violators and hold themselves accountable. They may need to ask someone to help with that. Perpetration can be a release of inner anxiety and fear, thus its roots need to be defined. Anger operates like a drug, so it has benefits that need to be released. In place of anger is the raw emotion of pain. And that's what perpetrators have avoided. Therefore, leaving the cycle can be dramatically difficult.

Healing is a tender space that will lead to freedom but will require courage and support. Anger, rage, and control can be seen as an actual addiction that needs to be broken and offered the same resources accordingly.

For Jan to heal, she may need professional support or a recovery community. She needs people that can accept her when she admits the truth. And that will allow her to move beyond her "bad" behavior and heal the victim that lies underneath.

APPLY GRACE

#1. LOVE, VALUE & ACCEPTANCE

Jan was powerless as a victim in the past and now held false power to try to control others. What she needed is the power of grace. While her wounds were deep, in the here and now she could begin to declare a power statement to begin to soothe the shame and speak grace. For Jan, the challenge was not to use her power wrongly. She needed to be reminded that, despite her worst moments, she was loved, valued, and accepted by God. Jan could use a power statement: "Even if I have been negative and hurtful to people, I am loved, valued, and accepted by God." With this driving her core, she has a new way to manage life. Jan also needs to tap into the power of forgiveness that comes through genuine repentance.

Copyright Spirit of Life Recovery. All Rights Reserved.

Her worthiness is based on the cross, but because she has participated in violating ways, she needs to be honest with God.

#2. EXPECTATIONS

When we come to discover the darker parts of our character, it can be difficult to see. Jan could have filled herself with pride and refused to admit her failure. Or she could have punished herself to the point of not being able to receive grace. But through grace, Jan can come as she is. Her failure isn't a surprise to God, and there is no need for self-punishing. She is welcome at the cross, broken and in need. We don't come to the cross because we are good. This is where grace is grace.

#3. NEEDS & FEELINGS

Jan's emotional life had been in turmoil for many years. The original pain from her past had never been fully processed, which led her to disconnect from her emotions early in life. After leaving the abusive marriage, all her emotions were redirected into anger. Anger, while a natural response to hurt, became her primary emotion. It served as a defense mechanism, shielding her from deeper, more vulnerable feelings. However, anger, over time, hardened her heart, preventing her from truly connecting with her own emotional world.

Jan's journey to healing requires her to confront the anger that has been masking her true emotions. Beneath the surface of anger, there are feelings of hurt, rejection, sadness, and fear that need to be acknowledged and expressed. If she continues to react from anger, especially in conflict, she risks pushing others away and reinforcing unhealthy patterns. Instead, she needs to find her authentic emotions and express them with vulnerability and honesty.

For example, instead of resorting to defensive language or attempting to control the situation, Jan could begin to communicate her real feelings. If she feels rejected, she could express herself by saying, "I feel sad when you ignore me." By speaking from her true heart, Jan takes a step toward vulnerability and authentic connection. It opens the door for healthier communication, where both parties can address the underlying issues, rather than getting caught up in the surface-level reactions driven by anger.

Jan also needs to learn more about herself and understand what is happening underneath the surface. She will need to be more intentional in understanding her thought life. Once again, being honest with herself is most of the battle.

Not only does Jan need to confront people with her true feelings, but she will also need to be honest with the people she has hurt in the past, or will hurt in the future. She can express her real emotions in the moment and then apologize and try to make things right. This will require humility on her part, and it won't come easily at first. Admitting fault is dramatically difficult for someone in a perpetrator role, but it is the pathway to freedom. It will lead to healthy relationships in the long run, as the same people she pushed away will be drawn to her.

#4. I CAN RESPONSE

Most of Jan's life, she felt powerless. Later, the false power of anger she had gained made her miserable, even though it accomplished the job of not having to be re-violated. It separated her rather than connecting her with others. Her "I can" statements come through a heart that gets healed and redeemed. She can let herself off the hook. She can forgive herself. She can ask the people she hurt to forgive her too. But beyond that, Jan actually wants the ability to have healthy relationships. She wants to be able to find peace in relationships and find the gift of intimacy with her husband.

Jan's response goes something like this:

- I can ask others to forgive me.
- I can be honest with myself and others.
- I can live life in the truth of my needs and fears.
- I can ask for help when I need it.
- I can apologize when I fall back into cycles.
- I can learn to love.
- I can learn to be honest and intimate.
- I can learn to trust others in time.
- I can heal my wounds and trauma from the past.\
- I can give myself lots of grace to recognize why I act the way I do.

Healing from multiple roles in the cycle can feel overwhelming. Having to admit being a perpetrator can sometimes be the hardest task of all. It's helpful to remember that at the cross, each one of us is a perpetrator. Each one of us has sinned and fallen short of God's standard. Thus, we all house shame for that. Each one of us needs grace. God isn't shocked by the status of the perpetrator; it's the very reason He came. It's just a matter of our ability to be honest with Him about it that determines the outcome.

APPLY:

Use this model in your own relational struggle. Identify the current cycle you are in and how you feel you are a perpetrator. Then work through the following:

- Who am I struggling with in relationship where I am a perpetrator? What do I do, and why do I do it?
- What is the original pain that drives my anger? Can I see both the anger and the pain?
- What is my power statement to secure my worth and identity in Jesus?
- Can I admit my wrongdoing?

Application:
Communicating Needs & Feeling (Page 64)
Boundaries (Page 65)

COMMUNICATING NEEDS & FEELINGS

Needs are the driving force within a relational dynamic. They are the unspoken language of the heart that drive us to act and respond. Finding our needs is one of the hardest things we'll be asked to do. That's why it's important we develop a needs assessment relationship to relationship. Many times, we don't where to begin. But if we can take some time to learn our needs, we can take action and create boundaries to manage them.

Here are some common needs, but there are many more in specific and relevant ways to our unique situation. Only use this as a guidelines, and then take a separate piece of paper to develop your relationship need inventory:

- the need for value (primary)
- the need for acceptance (primary)
- the need for leadership
- the need for respect
- the need for support
- the need for appreciation
- the need to be seen and known
- the need for fun and joy
- the need for security and safety
- the need for affirmation

- the need for encouragement
- the need for understanding
- the need for grace
- the need for physical touch
- the need for love
- the need for protection
- the need for material resources
- the need for social interaction
- the need for dreams
- the need for hope

Expressing a need is as simple as "I need this (name the need)." I need" is a communicated statement that specifically offers a pathway for someone else to respond to us. We can ask this with kindess, resect and gentleness. We cannot use our needs as a license to be demanding, controlling or punishing. Once we attach a need to shame, it is no longer healthy.

DEFINING THE NEED
What is my need? Where does it come from? Can God meet this need? Is it appropriate to ask _____ _____ for this need? If no, we work with God to help us process this need and to heal the space of our heart where that need may not have been met previously.

COMMUNICATING THE NEEDS & FEELINGS
1. When my need is _____, I can express the need outrightly. I do not have to imply or expect _____ to figure out my need for me. Speaking my needs is healthy.
2. If my needs or feelings are rejected or misunderstood, I can bring it to God. I can't force _____ to understand or meet my needs.
3. I can present my needs and feelings to God. He is interested and will hear me. He will help me.
4. If my need remains unmet, I can pray and ask God to help me or to redefine the need. I can ask for healing. I can ask for other resources.
5. I can set boundaries when people intentionally withdraw needs or bring extreme relational pain by not providing a need. Specifically, I set a boundary with _____.

Copyright Spirit of Life Recovery. All Rights Reserved.

BOUNDARIES

Log the boundary dynamics that affect you in a day to day basis to start re-wiring from a state of powerlessness to all powerful in Jesus!

MY ROLE	POWER STATEMENT	EXPECTATIONS	NEEDS & FEELING	I CAN

Copyright Spirit of Life Recovery. All Rights Reserved.

PART 5
Resolutions

We have already explored the concepts of expectations, needs, and "I can" statements. However, during times of crisis, we must engage in deeper communication and employ more advanced conflict resolution techniques that go beyond these foundational elements. While establishing boundaries and adopting healthy ways of reacting can bring significant shifts in our lives, there are moments when we need to dig even deeper. The truth is that mending relationships becomes increasingly difficult when longstanding patterns have been established over time. Therefore, we must confront these dynamics head-on, make decisions, and seek resolutions that ultimately lead to peace amidst the turmoil.

The long-term benefit of living with grace-based boundaries isn't just about protecting ourselves from harm—it's about cultivating an environment where hope is restored, freedom is nurtured, and wholeness can unfold in God's timing. Without this internal transformation, we remain stuck in survival mode, repeating cycles instead of stepping into a new way of living.

Relationships can either bind or break us—but through the process of reconciliation, they can also become places of healing. Even when reconciliation isn't possible, we can still heal. However, healing isn't about becoming a polished, idealized version of who we think we should be. It's not about performing to meet unrealistic standards. True transformation comes when we experience the deep power of acceptance. It lifts us into a posture of surrender rather than striving. Grace begins its work in us—and from there, it flows through us. As grace anchors us, it disarms the power of shame, exposing it as a barrier to our true design.

Still, walking away from shame is not easy. In many ways, it behaves like an addiction—pulling us back into familiar, destructive patterns. Whether we perpetuate cycles of shame or find ourselves on the receiving end of someone else's dysfunction, the journey toward healing begins with awareness. When we learn to identify shame, assess it, and respond with grace instead of fear or control, we begin to loosen the grip of relational strongholds.

Shame-based relationships shape our hearts with false narratives of unworthiness. But when we approach those relationships with new strategies rooted in grace, we make space for transformation. That's why our final step in building grace-based boundaries involves learning to assess our expectations, clearly communicate our needs, and engage in healthy conflict resolution.

Yet, even with tools and strategies in place, we must always return to one truth: change is an inside job. We don't change others—we allow God to change us. When grace transforms our inner world, everything else begins to shift. And if we find ourselves feeling weak, insecure, or unsure along the way, we don't shame ourselves. We return to our need, rest in the healing love of Jesus, and

Copyright Spirit of Life Recovery. All Rights Reserved.

let His grace meet us personally. Because, at the end of the day, solving our relationships is not the main thing—it is allowing Jesus to restore our hearts.

POWER DIFFERENTIAL

Relationships shaped by shame-based dynamics can be incredibly difficult to understand—especially when power and control are involved. One reason for this complexity is that discerning who is "right" or "wrong" often feels confusing and unclear. Shame clouds our ability to interpret reality, making it harder to see the full picture.

When we begin to feel that someone's behavior is so out of alignment that it requires serious boundaries or change, we must pause and be sober-minded in our assessment. Jesus reminded us of this principle when He taught, "Why do you see the speck in your brother's eye, but do not notice the log in your own eye? ... First take the log out of your own eye, and then you will see clearly to take the speck out of your brother's eye" (Matthew 7:3-5). This scripture encourages us to examine our own faults before judging others, ensuring that our perspective remains balanced and humble.

However, for many—especially those with past trauma—the opposite may occur. We might shrink ourselves, internalize blame, and allow someone else's truth to dictate our reality. This dynamic is especially potent when there is a power differential, where one person holds a position of authority or influence over the other.

Power differentials can manifest in many forms: between a parent and child, a pastor and congregant, or a boss and employee. While it's natural to honor those in leadership, we must also recognize that positions of authority can sometimes be wielded through a distorted lens. It is painful and disorienting when someone we trust misuses their power to control or silence us.

In these moments, we must return to the one lens that always guides us rightly—God's truth. His truth reminds us that we are not defined by our roles or the opinions of others. We are not meant to see ourselves as inherently flawed or as having the right to dictate others' experiences. Likewise, being in a vulnerable position doesn't make us victims without agency.

The key to healing these dynamics lies in freedom and grace. Every relationship must allow space for both individuals to be led by God and to grow in His light. When one person begins to dictate how the other should think, feel, or act, the essential freedom needed for genuine connection starts to erode. Where freedom is lost, relationships break down.

Unhealthy dynamics form when control replaces connection. To assess the health of our relationships, we must ask ourselves: How much freedom do I feel to listen to God, to grow, and to express my true self? And how much control—either given or taken—exists within my relationships?

When we tolerate patterns of control—whether we are the ones exerting it or enduring it—we stray from the grace that God intends for our lives. True, healthy connection is built on mutual respect, personal freedom, and the humility to continue growing together. This is the foundation on which resilient, compassionate relationships are built—a reminder that every person is meant to thrive in an environment of love and understanding.

Copyright Spirit of Life Recovery. All Rights Reserved.

BOTTOM LINES

Every relationship carries a degree of pain and challenge. However, pain alone does not define a bottom line. Pain is part of growth, and conflict is part of learning. A bottom line, on the other hand, helps us define the "I can't" space in a relationship—the point at which something crosses a threshold that our heart and soul can no longer bear without harm.

We don't define bottom lines to give up prematurely or to assume the worst. Rather, we define them so that everything that isn't a bottom line can be addressed through boundaries, conflict resolution, and communication. Without defining what we can't bear, we risk absorbing everything—leading to feelings of continual violation, confusion, and betrayal.

A bottom line is not an accusation; it is an act of clarity. It is, in many ways, an admission of love and value. It says, "I care about you. I see your worth. But I can no longer live in this dynamic without being deeply harmed." When we focus solely on how a person should change or who we think they should be, we slip into a shame-driven posture. However, when we define bottom lines from a place of love, we are not just protecting ourselves; we are also honoring the other person's humanity.

At the heart of a bottom line lies this question: How much harm can I carry before I lose myself? This is not a question of judgment; it is one of internal truthfulness. If we don't clarify our limits, we will continue to allow cycles that erode trust and sabotage connection.

It is important to note that most relationships will not have many bottom lines. These should not be used as threats or ultimatums, nor should they be announced every time we are upset. They are private, prayerful understandings of what our heart can no longer endure.

There is no formula for when to stay or when to leave. There is no one-size-fits-all solution. Each relationship comes with different standards and thresholds. For example, marriage carries the sacred bond of covenant, which calls for deep levels of grace and endurance. However, covenant does not mean giving permission for anything. Even in marriage, there are situations—such as repeated sexual unfaithfulness—that may become bottom-line issues requiring more serious intervention.

HOW TO DRAW A BOTTOM LINE

Defining a bottom line does not mean closing the door completely. In fact, bottom lines should be paired with two powerful elements: a grace bridge and an exit plan.

1. THE GRACE BRIDGE

A grace bridge is a path toward restoration. It says, "If you are willing to admit this harm and take responsibility for it, I am willing to walk toward healing with you." This is the very heart of God—a desire to reconcile and redeem. A grace bridge offers hope and honors the potential for change.

2. THE EXIT PLAN

An exit plan is the other side of the boundary. It says, "If nothing changes, if there is no acknowledgment or desire to make this right, I will take this step to protect my peace and safety." This could mean separation, distance, or ending the relationship, depending on the circumstances. The exit plan doesn't come from anger—it comes from clarity. It ensures we don't remain trapped in toxic or destructive cycles when change is not possible.

When we draw bottom lines, we are not choosing control; we are choosing to maintain our own heart space. We are choosing to honor our God-given worth and love others in truth, not in enabling silence. Bottom lines are not punishments; they are invitations—first to ourselves and then to others—to live in wholeness and grace.

NEXT LEVEL BOUNDARIES

Next-level boundaries are not about punishment; they serve to clearly define what is no longer sustainable and establish what is necessary for a relationship to survive. Rather than drawing harsh lines, these boundaries are drawn with love, signaling our commitment to a healthy, respectful connection.

When communication becomes destructive—whether through emotionally or spiritually wounding language, physical abuse, or substance abuse that leads to relational breakdown—it is necessary to set clear limits. Similarly, when trust is shattered by marital unfaithfulness, betrayal, spiritual toxicity, or when friendships become toxic with manipulation, gossip, or judgment, setting boundaries becomes essential to protect our well-being. In these moments, a boundary is more than just a rule; it is a direct request for change, offered with grace and a reasonable time-frame to see progress. It is an invitation to move toward healing and restoration—free from shame and threats, yet firm enough to honor our values.

For example, you might ask that addictive behaviors not be brought into the home, offer support for professional help, and allow time for recovery. Alternatively, you might create a temporary separation from someone whose abusive actions have caused harm, while keeping the door open for healing through counseling, sincere repentance, and ownership of harm. Setting financial boundaries with children or adult children can also be a loving way to connect support with responsibility and growth.

It is important to understand that a next-level boundary does not magically change someone or force them to engage differently. Instead, it simply clarifies the issue at hand and offers a bridge for change. If that bridge is ignored, the boundary becomes a line of consequence. However, if the boundary is never enforced, the bridge loses its strength, and the relationship may slowly drift back into dysfunction.

Defining these boundaries may sometimes require outside support—whether from trusted mentors, pastoral counsel, or professional guidance—to ensure we remain grounded in reason rather than driven by resentment. The most powerful part of setting a boundary begins with recognizing what truly belongs to us. As we have learned, boundaries start with self-awareness; they are not intended to control another's behavior but to protect our own space, safety, and peace.

It is also crucial to use next-level boundaries correctly. If a next-level boundary is used as a threat to change someone's behavior in situations that do not warrant such intervention, it can do tremendous damage. Misused, a next-level boundary becomes a tool of control. Even more harmful is when we punish someone for a trauma response rather than inviting them into a dialogue of understanding and compassion. Ultimately, our heart posture determines how we employ these boundaries. In their true form, next-level boundaries are about healing and reconciliation—not about making someone change on our terms.

Healthy boundaries use the language of grace rather than shame. They don't accuse or attack; they simply clarify. Firm, yet rooted in love, they express a deep care for the relationship. For example, one might say, "I love you, and I want better for us. You mean so much to me, which is why this behavior is damaging. When you [specific behavior], I feel [how it affects you]. I'm asking for [specific change], or I will need to [consequence]." This kind of language, tailored to the unique dynamics of each relationship, communicates honesty, dignity, and a genuine desire to move forward without manipulation—allowing us to walk in alignment with our values rather than our fears.

WHEN RELATIONSHIPS MUST END

There are times when relationships must end—not because we want them to, but because they have become harmful or unsustainable. While reconciliation is always the ideal, it isn't always possible, and we must be honest about that reality.

Some relationships become so rooted in denial, pride, or destructiveness that they leave no room for growth or connection. We may ask for change, but it never comes. We may extend grace, but it is never received. At a certain point, continuing the relationship as it is becomes an act of self-betrayal.

We must accept that, in some cases, walking away is the most loving and life-giving choice we can make. This doesn't mean we stop caring; it means we stop allowing ourselves to be harmed. We stop believing that our endurance can fix what only God can heal. We begin to focus on what we can actually change—our choices, our space, and our healing.

Staying in a relationship that continually depletes us while trying to force change will exhaust us. It binds us in the very cycle of pain we long to escape. Sometimes, the most courageous thing we can do is to release the relationship—to grieve what it was, honor what we hoped it would be, and trust God with what comes next.

That said, ending a relationship should not be our first response. Grace always offers a bridge. But when that bridge is repeatedly ignored or abused, we must face the truth: not every relationship can be saved. Even in those moments, God is present. He remains faithful. He continues the work of healing in our hearts, no matter what others choose.

There is wisdom in knowing that every relationship will involve some level of brokenness.

Copyright Spirit of Life Recovery. All Rights Reserved.

No person is perfect; no connection is without conflict. But when a relationship becomes destructive without repentance, it is not wrong to walk away. It is simply necessary.

And when we do so in grace—not out of bitterness or revenge—we preserve our integrity, protect our hearts, and open space for true restoration to begin.

WHEN WE STAY

While some relationships may eventually need to end, most will continue to have some form of connection. In these cases, choosing to stay is not simply about tolerating the status quo, but about contributing something new and different to the dynamic—even if the other person isn't. The decision to remain in a relationship, despite the challenges, means embracing the responsibility of change, personal growth, and transformation. It requires a willingness to evolve and step into new ways of communicating and engaging, even when the path forward feels uncertain or difficult.

This is especially important because, in many cases, shame has become deeply embedded in our relationships, poisoning the way we interact with one another. Shame distorts perceptions, drives destructive behaviors, and creates barriers that prevent genuine connection and understanding. Managing shame within these dynamics through grace can feel overwhelming. It's not simply about controlling our reactions or setting limits—it's about learning to engage with others from a place of wholeness, forgiveness, and love. This requires us to develop new skills, cultivate emotional resilience, and shift both our perspective and communication style to be more aligned with grace and empathy.

While we have already covered boundaries in Part 4, it is equally important to recognize that boundaries alone are not enough. To truly heal and break free from cycles of dysfunction, we must understand the nature of shame-based communication. Shame-based communication is insidious, often appearing in subtle, almost unconscious ways that perpetuate pain and misunderstanding. Recognizing its presence is the first step in addressing it effectively. We must learn to identify shame-driven patterns—whether in ourselves or others—so that we can dismantle them and create space for healthier, more compassionate ways of relating. By understanding how shame communicates and how it influences our responses, we can better navigate these relational challenges and create opportunities for real healing and growth.

SHAME-BASED COMMUNICATION

Judging: We assume we already understand someone's heart and intentions, reducing them to a single label. For example, saying, "You are…" without truly understanding their inner world.

Accusing: We charge someone with doing something wrong without clear evidence, like saying, "You are always doing this to me."

Assuming: We jump to conclusions about a person's emotions or character, e.g., "You're mad at me; I can tell," without asking or listening.

Guilting: We attempt to make others feel bad about their actions by saying, "You made me feel awful,"

Copyright Spirit of Life Recovery. All Rights Reserved.

hoping that their remorse will change the situation.

Labeling: Instead of seeing someone as a whole person, we reduce them to a negative condition, such as saying, "You are nothing but a narcissist."

Gas-lighting: We dismiss or invalidate another's feelings by calling them "crazy" or "sick in the head for thinking that," making them question their own reality.

Blaming: We assign fault entirely to another, declaring, "You are to blame," without considering the full complexity of the situation.

Criticizing: We focus solely on the negatives, pointing out every perceived error with statements like, "You always do this wrong."

Over-correcting: We try to manage someone's behavior by insisting they do things "the right way," even without being asked, e.g., "You need to do it this way."

Threatening: We use the fear of punishment to provoke change, saying, "If you don't [do something], you'll pay the price."

Punishing: We resort to harming or seeking revenge on someone for not meeting our expectations, such as saying, "You'll get what you deserve for [not doing something]."

These communication styles, fueled by shame, can make interactions explosive and dysfunctional. They create an environment where true understanding and connection become nearly impossible.

GRACE

Grace offers an entirely different approach. Rather than reacting with judgment or blame, grace encourages us to allow feelings and needs to be expressed openly. It invites us to acknowledge that while differences exist, they do not have to tear us apart. Instead of demanding immediate agreement or change, grace suggests we work through our differences with dialogue aimed at deep understanding.

Consider asking questions such as:

"Help me understand what you need and what you feel."

"Can you share your perspective?"

"Why do you think or feel that way?"

These questions are not about assigning blame or proving a point—they are about exploring the honest needs and feelings of each person. It's important to remember that these expressions are not unchangeable facts but rather windows into what is happening inside two hearts.

Copyright Spirit of Life Recovery. All Rights Reserved.

For example:

- Instead of saying, "You never support me," grace says, "Lately I've been feeling unsupported. Can we talk about how we might show up for each other better?"
- Instead of snapping, "You're always so distant," grace says, "I miss feeling close to you. Is something on your mind?"
- Instead of reacting with, "You just don't care," grace says, "When I don't hear back from you, I start to feel invisible. I'd like to feel more connected."
- Instead of shutting down during an argument, grace says, "I want to work through this, but I'm feeling overwhelmed. Can we take a break and come back to this later?"
- Instead of demanding, "You better change or I'm done," grace says, "I value this relationship, and I need to feel safe and heard. Are you willing to work on this with me?"

At its core, using the language of grace is about fostering intimacy. It means connecting with another person first, without rushing to correct, condemn, or change their point of view. Through this type of connection, we allow ourselves to truly see into someone else's inner world and invite them to see into ours.

While this approach carries the risk of vulnerability and even rejection, it also offers the best opportunity for authentic relationships. By choosing to replace shame-based communication with grace, we open up a path to mutual growth and deeper connection—even when it feels challenging to take that first step. (See worksheet: Activating Grace at the end of this section).

RESOLVING CONFLICT

When someone sees the same situation from another point of view, we don't have to be angry. Using threats, labels, or punishment for disagreement is the role of shame. Instead, we can learn to ask more questions, get more information, and seek to clarify our own part. We don't assume that someone understands us or knows what we need. Thus, we can express our own needs and feelings:

I feel/need _____ .
When you _____, it makes me feel _____.

It's tempting to revert to shame strategies if our feelings or needs are minimized. We might respond with words such as, "You never listen to me," "You don't care about me," or "You are a selfish jerk." Any time we use "you" statements, we are likely using shame. This is a hard habit to break because, in cycles of pain, most of the activity centers around the wrongdoing of others. Accepting that people won't always meet our needs or understand our feelings is where we lay our weapons down and find the safety to process that with Jesus. We can depart from conversations where our point of view isn't valued. Someone who uses our needs and feelings as weapons against us—or overtly isn't interested in our wellbeing—may require Next-level boundaries.

If we've operated in shame in relationships, we can't expect everyone to change overnight. In fact, at first it isn't even about whether the other person responds right or wrong. It's about learning for ourselves how to change the atmosphere of the relationship. It may or may not affect the outcomes for the other person, but the immediate benefit is that we dislodge shame's influence in our own heart.

Conflict is inevitable in any relationship—but when handled well, it can become a doorway to deeper understanding and connection. Grace-based conflict resolution means addressing issues without resorting to shame, retaliation, or avoidance. It begins by seeing conflict not as a threat, but as an invitation to grow.

Key principles of grace-based conflict resolution include:

- Stay curious: Instead of reacting, pause and ask, "What might really be going on here?"
- Seek mutual understanding: Each person has a valid perspective, even if we don't agree.
- Own your part: Begin by acknowledging your own needs, triggers, and patterns. "I realize I may have…" creates a non-defensive tone.
- Practice active listening: Reflect back what you hear. "What I hear you saying is…" helps ensure clarity and mutual respect.
- Stay present: Don't bring up every past grievance. Focus on the present moment and how to move forward.
- Name the impact, not the character: Instead of "You are selfish," say, "When this happened, I felt overlooked."
- Agree on the process: Sometimes resolution doesn't come instantly. It's okay to say, "Let's take a break and come back to this when we both feel calm."

Resolution is less about fixing every disagreement and more about restoring connection. Grace reminds us that reconciliation is often a process, not a single moment.

RECONCILIATION THROUGH GRACE

True reconciliation happens when both individuals commit to the healing process. It begins with a shared willingness to face past wounds, take responsibility for personal failures, and choose grace over shame. This isn't a one-sided act but a mutual journey that clears unspoken resentment, breaks silence, and interrupts cycles of hurt.

Reconciliation invites us to see each other through God's standard of love. Though we may never fully meet every need, we can still choose grace instead of criticism. In this space, manipulation and grudges give way to honest, tender communication and a desire for unity over being right.

Grace doesn't demand perfection—it asks for a soft, compassionate heart. It says, "I see your flaws, and I still choose connection. I see your wounds, and I will not add to them." This is the language of healing, where pain is honored and new beginnings are made possible.

STEPS TO HEALING TOGETHER

1. Mutual Acknowledgment

Reconciliation begins with each person humbly examining their part in the hurt. This requires sincere self-reflection, confession without blame, and a heart open to God's grace. Rather than pointing fingers, we invite healing by recognizing our humanity and seeking forgiveness with compassion.

2. Releasing Blame

Healing requires letting go of blame—not to excuse harm, but to release resentment and open space for empathy. As we forgive like Christ forgives us (Ephesians 4:32), we free ourselves from the burden of bitterness and make room for meaningful dialogue and restoration.

3. Choosing Grace

Grace replaces judgment with compassion, criticism with understanding, and retribution with the willingness to rebuild. Forgiveness can be extended individually, but reconciliation truly thrives when grace flows mutually.

4. Clear and Loving Communication

Effective healing requires expressing feelings and needs with honesty and care, avoiding blame or manipulation. Graceful dialogue creates a safe space for healing:

"I love you and want better for us. When voices are raised, I feel overwhelmed. Can we try to speak calmly or pause when needed?"

"I care about you. When I hear dismissive comments, I feel discouraged. Can we agree to listen fully before responding?"

"I value us. When discussions end harshly, I feel isolated. Can we take a short break and pray before continuing?"

5. Affirming Worth

Seeing one another through God's eyes transforms our healing process. A simple affirmation like, "Your pain matters to me, and I'm here with compassion," reminds the other person of their value.

Reconciliation nurtures not only our own healing but the healing of those we love.

6. Allowing Time for Growth

Healing takes time. Whether through counseling, recovery, or gradual change, every step forward matters. Patience reflects trust in God's timing, giving space for lasting transformation and letting grace into the very fibers of our being.

Reconciliation, when it occurs, is one of the most precious gifts we can experience. It is healing made visible, restoration in motion, and the fruit of grace taking root in two hearts simultaneously. While forgiveness may be a personal act, true reconciliation is mutual. We cannot force another to heal; we can only be ready to embrace that healing when it arises naturally between us.

Ultimately, grace is the only foundation strong enough to hold a lasting relationship. It is the force powerful enough to repair what shame has destroyed and the unmistakable mark of God's presence in our connections. By choosing reconciliation, we open ourselves to a future where relationships

Copyright Spirit of Life Recovery. All Rights Reserved.

are not defined by past pain but by the promise of renewal, mutual respect, and deep, abiding love.

Application:
Bottom Lines Worksheet (Page 78)
Conflict Resolution (Page 79)
Catching Shame and Activating Grace (Page 80)

Boundaries & Breaking Cycles of Pain

BOTTOM LINES

We can choose the place in the relationship where something has to change for us to continue. It should be fair and reasonable and align with God's heart. We can't ask that a person change; but we can set a limit or consequence for the continuation of something extremely painful. We don't just think these out in a moment, but may need time to absorb and pray over these areas. Preplanning helps us to avoid triggers or blow outs from built up offenses.

In my relationship with _____, I set the following bottom line.

When _____ does/says _____ OR

When _____ does/says _____

I need to make the following change (example: ask them to move out temporarily, put the relationship on pause, relinquish financial support, etc.)
_____

Have I offered a bridge? If so, what is it? If there is no bridge, how can _____ repair or participate in redemption? Am I being fair and reasonable? Does this bridge match God's heart? Am I sure? If I can't find a bridge, then I have no right to set a strong boundary.
_____
_____
_____

If the bottom line isn't repaired through a bridge, am I willing, to follow through on the next level boundary or simply let go? _____. If not, then I'm not ready to draw a bottom line.

COMMUNICATING A BOTTOM LINE:
I don't have to mean or rude in communicating a bottom line and developing a level boundary. I can be decent. If I'm emotional, angry or triggered, I need to wait to express my bottom line.

When I communicate a bottom line, I can:
- Express the positive reasons I need to set this boundary
- Express my interest in retaining a better/healthier relationship
- Express why the behavior is so harmful to me
- Express why I need to set the boundary
- Express my desire for the relationship to work, but my commitment to enforcing a bottom line.
- Use "I" language and minimize shame dialogue

I need to wait/pause/pray when:
- I'm unsure or not serious about the bottom line, I should not communicate it.
- Using the bottom line to threaten or intimate
- The bottom line doesn't match God's heart
- I'm operating from anger or in a trigger
- I'm operating in shame

Copyright Spirit of Life Recovery. All Rights Reserved.

CONFLICT RESOLUTION WORKSHEET

Stay curious: Instead of reacting, pause and ask, "What might really be going on here?"

_____
_____
_____
_____

Seek mutual understanding: Each person has a valid perspective, even if we don't agree. What's mine? What's theirs?

_____
_____
_____
_____

Own your part: Begin by acknowledging your own needs, triggers, and patterns. "I realize I may have…" creates a non-defensive tone.

_____
_____
_____
_____

Practice active listening: Reflect back what you hear. "What I hear you saying is…" helps ensure clarity and mutual respect.

_____
_____
_____
_____

Stay present: Don't bring up every past grievance. Focus on the present moment and how to move forward.

_____
_____
_____
_____

Name the impact, not the character: Instead of "You are selfish," say, "When this happened, I felt overlooked."

_____
_____

Copyright Spirit of Life Recovery. All Rights Reserved.

CATCHING SHAME & ACTIVATING GRACE

SHAME AWARENESS	GRACE ACTIVATION	SPECIFIC APPLICATION TO ME
Measuring (too good, not good enough)	I am enough based on who Jesus says I am (power statement)	
Judgment (finding fault)	Accept what is presented, seek truth to make decisions	
Accusing/Assuming (making a case to find someone guilty)	Ask questions, get information	
Making someone know they did something wrong.	Asking what a person needs or feels (expressing what you need or feel)	
Labeling — Identifying a person by what they do (real or perceived)	Seeing people and ourselves as lovable, valuable and acceptable (power statement)	
Gas-lighting — Calling someone crazy for feeling, thinking or behaving	Honoring individual perspectives; seeking to understand or be understood.	
Blaming (giving someone the burden of responsibility)	Seeking to understand personal responsibility	
Criticizing (fault finding)	Finding ways to affirm and ask for needs or feelings.	
Correcting (controlling)	Letting people make choices; setting boundaries	
Threatening (using fear to change someone)	Using boundaries that are firm	
Punishing: Getting revenge	Forgiving, setting boundaries	

Copyright Spirit of Life Recovery. All Rights Reserved.

PART 6
Made for More

The cycles of pain you have experienced—while real and painful—are not your destiny. They are not your definition. Things h*appened* to you, but they are not *you*. Often, we remain entangled in these patterns not because we want to, but because we have learned to function within them. In times of fear, loss, or rejection, survival becomes the strategy. It becomes the default posture we adopt to meet our basic need to be seen, loved, and safe.

But hear this: no matter what others have done or failed to do, you still have a choice. You are not powerless. You are not bound to live on repeat. You can turn your attention toward the One who authored your life and named your worth. You can reorient your heart to what is eternally true: *who God says you are.* You were made for more. Not more striving. Not more perfectionism. Not more desperate attempts to be chosen or kept. You were made for life in Christ—a life rooted in identity, shaped by love, and sustained by grace.

Your true self is not something you must invent or earn. It is something to uncover. It is the version of you that was formed in the heart of God before time began. It is the self that exists when shame has no voice and fear holds no dominion. It is who you are when grace becomes your home.

God has not called you to live from a fractured identity—one that fluctuates with circumstances, wounds, or others' opinions. You were not created to carry the weight of unmet expectations or to stay buried beneath unresolved pain. You were formed in love. You were made to live from love, not just in search of it.

The antidote to these cycles is not more control. It is grace—pure, powerful, transformative grace. Grace removes the need to control. Grace silences the accusations of shame. Grace invites you to come home to the person God has always seen. Grace allows you to confront pain with truth, not fear. It gives you the space to unlearn what trauma taught you and relearn what love has always said.

THE FOUNDATION OF GRACE IN RELATIONSHIPS

While we often try to extend grace to others, we must remember this foundational truth: grace must begin within. We cannot live out grace in relationships if we have not first received it for ourselves. Grace must become more than a theological idea—it must become a lived reality, a guiding posture in how we relate to ourselves and others.

When grace becomes your operating system—your baseline for thoughts, emotions, and choices—transformation unfolds. From that place, you begin to:

- See yourself as God sees you.
- Disengage from cycles of performance, codependency, and control.

Copyright Spirit of Life Recovery. All Rights Reserved.

- Establish boundaries rooted in dignity, not fear.
- Connect authentically without compromising who you are.
- Extend compassion without enabling dysfunction.

To walk in grace is not merely to be forgiven. It is to embrace a completely new way of being. It is to live from wholeness, not from wounds.

RECEIVING GRACE AS A LIFESTYLE

This journey is not instantaneous. It is gradual. It is formed in small, daily decisions of the heart. Learning to live from grace requires intentionality. It requires courage—the courage to pause and notice where shame still speaks, where fear still governs, and where old identities still linger.

Most of us were trained by survival. We learned to overachieve to be noticed, to overextend to be accepted, to stay silent to avoid abandonment. But survival is not the inheritance of a child of God. You were not created to merely endure—you were created to flourish.

And grace is the way forward. Grace is the daily, courageous act of surrender. It is choosing to believe what God says, even when the voices of the past are loud. It is returning, again and again, to who Jesus says you are.

As grace takes root in your heart, it brings with it a holy confrontation. You will begin to notice the lies you once believed. You will see how shame twisted your view of self. You will recognize the ways you've tried to protect yourself through control, denial, or over-functioning.

And in those moments, grace will invite you into freedom. Healing requires honesty. It invites us to revisit our stories with compassion, not judgment. To trace the origin of pain and allow God's redemptive love to rewrite the meaning. This process is not about emotional perfection, but about truthful alignment. It is choosing to believe heaven's version of your life over the version written by fear, trauma, or rejection.

THE PLEDGE OF GRACE

I am not lovable based on how others love me.
I am not valuable based on how others perceive me.
I am not acceptable based on how others receive me.

I am loved, valuable, and acceptable because God has called me His own.
My name is written in the Lamb's Book of Life.
I am fully known and fully seen by my Creator, and I am not forgotten.
He has called me by name, and He has formed me with purpose.

I do not control how others respond to me.
I cannot rewrite the past or erase its wounds.
But I can stand in the present, rooted in the truth of God's love.

Copyright Spirit of Life Recovery. All Rights Reserved.

I may fail. I may fall short. I may be rejected.
But none of these diminish my identity in Christ.
I do not belong to shame. I do not serve fear.
I am ruled by truth. I am governed by grace.

I lay down the tools of judgment, control, and self-protection.
I surrender the compulsion to perform, to rescue, or to strive.
I renounce the cycle of pain as my way of life.
In its place, I embrace the way of grace.

What I cannot do, I entrust to God.
Where I am weak, He is strong.
Where I am broken, He is healer.
Where I am lost, He is the way.

I do not partner with lies.
I partner with the Word of God, which is life and truth.
I believe that His plans for me are for my good.
That His mercy never runs out.
That His love cannot be outrun.

I remember today that others, too, are worthy of this same grace—even those who have wounded me.
I am free to love, free to release, and free to remain whole.

This is my new foundation.
This is the sound of my soul at rest.
This is the truth I will live by: I am loved. I am valued. I am accepted.

ROOTED IN HIS POWER AND LOVE

This rooted truth can summarize the totality of the transition from cycles of pain to the power of grace:

"I pray that from his glorious, unlimited resources he will empower you with inner strength through his Spirit. Then Christ will make his home in your hearts as you trust in him. Your roots will grow down into God's love and keep you strong. And may you have the power to understand, as all God's people should, how wide, how long, how high, and how deep his love is. May you experience the love of Christ, though it is too great to understand fully. Then you will be made complete with all the fullness of life and power that comes from God. Now all glory to God, who is able, through his mighty power at work within us, to accomplish infinitely more than we might ask or think. Glory to him in the church and in Christ Jesus through all generations forever and ever! Amen." — Ephesians 3:16–20

You were made for more.

www.ingramcontent.com/pod-product-compliance
Lightning Source LLC
Chambersburg PA
CBHW081507040426
42446CB00017B/3431